COLORADO'S DARING
IVY BALDWIN

Aviator, Aerialist & Aeronaut

DR. JACK STOKES BALLARD

Published by The History Press
Charleston, SC
www.historypress.com

Copyright © 2020 by Dr. Jack Stokes Ballard
All rights reserved

Back cover: Courtesy of History Colorado Collection.

First published 2020

Manufactured in the United States

ISBN 9781467146333

Library of Congress Control Number: 2020934362

Notice: The information in this book is true and complete to the best of our knowledge. It is offered without guarantee on the part of the author or The History Press. The author and The History Press disclaim all liability in connection with the use of this book.

All rights reserved. No part of this book may be reproduced or transmitted in any form whatsoever without prior written permission from the publisher except in the case of brief quotations embodied in critical articles and reviews.

This book is dedicated to my wife, Arleda, who, over sixty-five-plus years, ably and patiently supported my enduring interest in history and the writing of my books.

CONTENTS

Preface	7
1. A Daring Career Begins	9
2. Touring beyond the United States	19
3. Military Balloonist	35
4. Off to the Spanish-American War	48
5. Back to Denver	56
6. Airships and Airplanes	66
7. Eldorado Springs	77
Notes	93
Selected Bibliography	103
Index	107
About the Author	111

PREFACE

Many a word has been written about the man Ivy Baldwin.[1] His name appeared numerous times in newspapers and entertainment notices from San Francisco to Baltimore and especially in Quincy, Illinois, and Denver, Colorado. From 1890 to 1953, he achieved celebrity status as a premier American aerialist and aeronaut. As his reputation spread, he was known by thousands of average citizens who were amazed at his courageous exploits. People literally looked up to Ivy Baldwin because he skillfully performed in the air, whether as a tightrope walker, balloonist, tower diver, parachutist or aviator. His death-defying exhibitions attracted thousands of paying spectators, and he acted as the headliner for various amusement parks and summer celebrations. Like so many television, movie and music stars today, Ivy Baldwin, in his time, was an extraordinary and fearless entertainer.

As Ivy Baldwin's life story unfolds, however, one quickly learns that he was more than an entertainment celebrity—he was an aviation pioneer. From his initial time as a balloonist in traveling shows, through his time as a balloonist in the army and his experiences in the Spanish-American War, to his many crashes in airplanes, Ivy Baldwin had a serious vision of man successfully navigating across the sky. He built, tested and flew balloons, dirigibles and airplanes. In addition, he earnestly sought to improve balloons and their support equipment. Pragmatically, he explored and participated in attempts at aerial photography, the assessment of

Preface

Ivy Baldwin as a young man, pictured about the time he toured as a balloonist and entertainer with the Baldwin Brothers Show. *History Colorado Collection.*

air currents and the means of obtaining directional flight. As a daring experimenter, he eventually established a number of aviation firsts.

The combination in one man of a consummate and celebrated entertainer and a pragmatic experimenter and pioneering participant in the fast-developing flight vehicles of the time made Ivy Baldwin a complex, interesting and unusual individual. However, his exploits, exciting as they were in the newspapers, did not fully define Baldwin's character and especially his notable contributions to the beginning of man's ability to fly. I hope this biography fills that void while telling the story of Ivy Baldwin's remarkable career.

A deliberate attempt has been made to incorporate the colorful newspaper descriptions of Ivy Baldwin's performances and his near-death experiences. At the same time, care has been taken in assessing the accuracy of comments, as many errors and contradictions arose when comparing articles. Ivy Baldwin's scrapbook, held by the History Colorado Museum library, served as a starting point for Ivy Baldwin research. The scrapbook contained news clippings that Baldwin collected over many years.

The Denver Public Library, the Friends of Historic Fort Logan Archives, Colorado Aviation Historical Society Archives and the Wings Over the Rockies Air and Space Museum Research Library provided important material and offered kind assistance in research and writing. Especially appreciated assistance came from Wendy Hall at the Carnegie Library for Local History of the Boulder Public Library and Nancy C. Dixon at the Quincy Museum in Quincy, Illinois. Ron Newberg, George Paxton and Judy Zelio reviewed the manuscript and offered critical and valuable comments that strengthened and improved this biography of Ivy Baldwin.

—Jack Stokes Ballard

1

A DARING CAREER BEGINS

He knew absolutely nothing about a balloon, but he had the nerve, and that is the stuff that aeronauts are made of.
—Houston Daily Post, *1905*

The impressive list included acrobat, aeronaut, balloonist, parachute jumper, trapeze artist, tightrope walker, entertainer and aviator. Those were some of the titles assigned to one man, the legendary Ivy Baldwin. Also, citizens from many other countries, and especially those from the state of Colorado, attached to those titles such colorful descriptive terms as reckless, crazy, daring and courageous. While Ivy Baldwin truly earned all those titles, they did not fully capture Ivy Baldwin the man. He had a unique personality and was an individual whom many never knew. Without a doubt, in the late nineteenth and early twentieth centuries, Ivy Baldwin, the master of so many entertaining aerial acts, reigned at or near the top of the United States' professional aeronauts. Few believed he could be surpassed in his aerial artistry and achievements, and they made him famous in his time and for the following generations.[2]

Born in Houston, Texas, on July 31, 1866, the fourth son of John H. and Elizabeth Ivy, the future "Ivy Baldwin" entered the world as William Ivy. In the family, he would always be called Willie. Little is known about his early childhood in south Texas, other than that he was a newsboy and shined shoes. As the years passed, he remained small in stature but very athletic.[3] He would never exceed five foot three and one-half inches and 112 pounds. Ivy's wiry, slender frame and wide-eyed face with very dark, bushy eyebrows gave him a long-enduring boyish appearance. Noted author Gene Fowler said Ivy had "squirrel-shooter eyes," meaning they were intense and piercing.[4] Perhaps the early arrival of a mustache helped establish that he had reached manhood. He lacked large, well-defined or articulated muscles, but he was especially strong. Very early, using his remarkable balance and body flexibility, he demonstrated gymnastic skills.[5] He would put his size and these notable physical attributes to advantage as he rapidly evolved into a circus acrobat and trapeze performer.

Ivy ran away from his Houston home when he was thirteen.[6] He claimed that his father beat him as a reason for leaving the family.[7] He went to San Antonio and sold the *San Antonio Express* newspaper. One time, while watching a man walk the tightrope, he determined to try the stunt. He even did a walk across the San Antonio River. Later, while crossing a lake near Pedro Springs,[8] he caught the eye of the owner of the Thayer-Noyes Circus. Hired on the spot, he then traveled with the circus and reportedly could do seven acts a day, quickly becoming one of the best performers. Later, he toured with the Sells Brothers Circus and soon developed into a more rounded showman by adding acrobatic and trapeze acts. Ivy often used an assumed billing name, as he feared his parents might pursue him. His early departure from his home and his subsequent circus performances reflected his adventuresome spirit and a strong desire to try almost anything. An element of wanderlust, appropriate for the circus shows, would dominate many years in Ivy's life.

Ivy's daring acts caused many injuries. He suffered a broken ankle and ribs at Wichita Falls, Texas, in 1882, when a drunk rode a horse into some men holding his tightrope guywires.[9] Regardless of injuries, Ivy enjoyed the itinerant lifestyle and the attention he received in a traveling circus show.

One of Ivy's favorite stories of his early years—and he had many of them—concerned a tightrope walk in Baltimore. During a Shriners' convention, he was to do a wire walk from 120 feet over a street. After the first performance, he encountered the police, who informed him that the city had an ordinance banning any aerial act without a safety net under it. He received a fine of five dollars. Ivy then went to the port docks, bought an old fishing net and laid it on the pavement under the wire for the next day's exhibition. He succeeded in avoiding another fine, and he delighted in claiming that he had out-foxed the police and city authorities.[10]

Ivy expanded his circus skills to balloon ascensions, and he claimed that he made his first balloon ascension in Terre Haute, Indiana, in 1879.[11] He described his introduction to ballooning this way: "One of the regular men with the circus that used to make the balloon ascension, he got on a drunk, didn't show up, so the manager asked me if I could go up and I went up with the balloon, and after that I took to ballooning."[12]

Later, a Houston newspaper interview made the observation that "he knew absolutely nothing about a balloon, but he had the nerve, and that is the stuff that aeronauts are made of."[13] Indeed, Ivy would become noted for his nerve, a characteristic that attracted paying spectators.

The fearless adolescent William Ivy soon caught the attention of two other circus showmen, brothers Tom and Sam Baldwin. Thomas Scott Baldwin acted as a leader and star performer for the Baldwin Brothers troupe, while Samuel Yates Baldwin often served in a more supportive way, such as fueling a balloon.[14] The Baldwins knew about a rising and talented young acrobat named William Ivy through contacts with many of their circus colleagues. Tom Baldwin had actually worked with Ivy as an acrobat in 1883. They decided to recruit Ivy as a Baldwin show tightrope walker, trapeze performer and balloonist. They wrote to Ivy, proposing that they form an exhibition team. William Ivy was receptive to the Baldwin proposal, which would lead to becoming virtually a partner. He reported to the Baldwin Brothers headquarters and Baldwin home in Quincy, Illinois, in the fall of 1889. Very quickly, Tom Baldwin and Ivy combined various stunts and soon added dramatic parachuting from a balloon.[15]

Thomas Baldwin, manager of the Baldwin Brothers show, had already earned a reputation as an outstanding aeronaut in the United States. Furthermore, his athletic appearance impressed crowds along with his daring acts. An English journalist described Tom Baldwin as "a clean-limbed, well-built man, evidently of enormous muscular strength, and in the best of health."[16] At five feet ten inches tall and approximately 180 pounds, he had a far sturdier physique than Ivy.

Like Ivy, Thomas Baldwin started performing as an acrobat and slack wire walker. He first achieved widespread fame with an 1885 slack wire walk of seven hundred feet from Cliff House to Seal Rock over the roiling sea near San Francisco. He then turned to balloon ascensions and, even later, daredevil parachuting acts from balloons. His development of a flexible parachute used in balloon ascensions "stimulated in turn the revival of an earlier phase of aeronautics—the use of the hot-air balloon."[17] Tom Baldwin's many experiences with balloons earned him at least one noteworthy label as a "Columbus of the Air."[18]

Unfortunately, by 1889, Thomas Baldwin had gained considerable weight and was over two hundred pounds. This constituted a particular problem in balloon ascensions and parachuting.[19] Recruiting the slight Ivy, who was six years younger than Tom, made good business sense. Furthermore, Ivy already possessed some parachuting skills, so he immediately became a featured performer.

It was during this time that William Ivy assumed the name Ivy Baldwin. In a much later interview, Ivy commented, "My right name is William Ivy, but I took that name Baldwin, I think it was 1887. Somewhere along there. I forgot the date I really did take the name."[20] The year seems to be 1889, when Ivy went to Quincy. According to Ivy, the primary reason for the name change was because "they didn't want the third man to be any different so we just made it all three Baldwins. We were doing acts then, you know, you've seen the flying trapeze."[21] In time, Tom Baldwin took on a role as manager, while Ivy became the star performer.[22]

Balloon ascensions had been around for a long time, and by the 1880s and 1890s, they had occurred in most regions of the United States. The history of such dramatic aerial events and the enduring public fascination with them stretched back to the Montgolfier brothers in France in 1783. Americans quickly came into the ballooning picture. On December 1, 1783, Benjamin Franklin, in France at the time, observed the first ascension of a man in a balloon. Like so many others, he was intrigued with what he saw and wrote about such startling aeronautical activity. Franklin wrote to Sir Joseph Banks, president of the Royal Society in London, commenting, "All well satisfied and delighted with the success of the experiment, and amusing one another with discourses of the various uses it may possibly be applied to." Prophetically, Franklin further added, "Among the pleasantries conversation produces on the subject, some suppose flying to be now invented, and that since men may be supported in the air, nothing is wanted but some light handy instrument to give and direct motion."[23] Ivy Baldwin and Tom Baldwin, along with many others, would strive to find some way to "give and direct motion," as noted by Franklin, but they had found use of balloons in another way—public entertainment.

Balloons at the time of the Baldwins were mostly crude vehicles and were often constructed by performers themselves. For example, Ivy Baldwin and his wife made some of his balloons. When asked what his balloons were made of, Ivy replied, "They were made of sea-island cotton. Yes, something like a bed sheet." He continued, "Then we put them over a stack and built a fire in the trench and let the soot stop up the pores, you

Ivy Baldwin stands on the right edge of a balloon basket just before an ascent. *History Colorado Collection.*

know. When we got them stopped up, then we've got a good balloon that will go up about 3,000 feet." As Ivy noted, the cotton sheet balloon was usually fueled by a fire via a fifteen-foot-long trench, and this "chimney" would feed the hot air to the balloon.[24]

Gas-filled balloons, most often with hydrogen produced by a combination of iron filings and sulfuric acid, were in use during this time, but the hot-air balloon proved most popular. The main reason was simple: hot-air balloons were cheaper to operate. Also, the exhibition balloonists found that it was easier to inflate the hot-air variety, and furthermore, they could recover the deflated bags with less inconvenience. Another factor was the ease with which a new recruit could operate the hot-air balloon. A raw recruit, like Ivy Baldwin, could learn hot-air balloon operation without knowing much about the science of aeronautics, while a gas balloon required more careful training.[25]

Controlling a balloon began with a mesh net over the top and dangling ropes with as many as twenty men tethering the gas bag while it filled. As the balloon was readied to rise, you could drop sandbags or ballast from the basket to produce the desired lift. A valve at the top could be opened to allow release of the hot air to descend. Balloonists were at the mercy of the wind, however, to go sideways after the men released the ropes.

Ivy Baldwin added more drama to his ascensions by dangling from a released rope. To the spectator, this appeared as if a man tethering the balloon had accidentally gotten entangled in the rising balloon's ropes. Ivy would sometimes hang thirty feet below the balloon on one rope and then climb up the rope and enter the basket when the balloon rose to three thousand feet.[26]

Men like Ivy and Tom Baldwin were always showmen and entertainers. They fully realized when the ascensions became stale and they needed to add gimmicks to retain the interest of paying customers. One new twist to the ascension was a trapeze act on a bar suspended below the basket. Parachuting from the balloon produced still another thrill. Parachuting had, at one time, been popular with spectators in Europe and the United States. When Tom Baldwin performed with impresario Park A. Van Tassel, they decided to revive the parachuting stunt.

While performing during the winter in San Francisco, Tom Baldwin experimented with parachute designs. On January 30, 1887, ready to do a test, he made a highly publicized parachute jump. The first parachute drops were from tethered balloons, and later, Tom Baldwin became one of the first to do one from a free-floating balloon. It was the July 4 celebration in his hometown, Quincy, Illinois, however, when he established his reputation for his parachuting skills. Baldwin reported that he had engaged six women to sew and stitch nine hundred yards of canvas at a cost of $1,000 to create a ninety-foot-high special balloon labeled "City of Quincy" for the big civic event. Further, he had fabricated a parachute of twenty-six feet in diameter with a five-foot-diameter wicker basket below. The day before the main festival, balloon inflation began from a city gas main, and the next morning, the balloon was moved by wagon to Quincy's Singleton Park. Tom Baldwin, dressed in a gray business suit, first announced the ascension and parachute drop would be postponed because of wind, greatly angering some eight to ten thousand spectators. Assessing the mood of the crowd, Baldwin decided to go ahead with the performance. After some frightening problems with men releasing the circle of retaining ropes and the discharge of ballast, the balloon rose rapidly. At more than four thousand feet, Baldwin made his drop, and the crowd grew silent. The descent took only three minutes and twenty seconds, but it provided the excitement for the patriotic day.[27]

This Tom Baldwin parachute jump brought new personal fame, helped revive regional and national interest in ballooning exhibitions and provided an important pattern for Ivy Baldwin. Ivy would learn and copy this episode as he became a member of the Baldwin Brothers show, and he used it as a template for his own exhibitions later.

Ivy believed that Tom had made the first parachute drops, but he claimed that he was among the first parachutists, asserting he had also done so in 1887.[28]

The early Baldwin parachute, in some ways, resembled the outline of a balloon. The canopy of muslin with a diameter of eighteen to twenty-one feet had a six-inch hole at the top. The bottom was held open by a hoop, preventing the chute's collapse.[29]

Ivy stated that he designed his own parachute of a twenty-two-foot-diameter billowing cloth. He used an attached dangling harness after determining that many jumpers had constructed their chutes like umbrellas, which then caused broken ribs in stiff winds.[30]

When someone asked Ivy how he knew a parachute would work, he replied, "We'd take a sandbag equal to our weight and take it up in the balloon and fasten that sandbag onto the parachute and then we'd throw the whole business out of the basket and one of us would stay down below and see how heavy it would hit the ground."[31]

Ivy, who would sometimes momentarily hang on the trapeze by his knees and then his feet, described his maneuver to the parachute: "I'd climb up

Ivy Baldwin entertains spectators during a hot-air balloon ascension by hanging by his feet beneath the basket. *Carnegie Library for Local History, Boulder, Colorado.*

there, this rope, up to the trapeze bar and then I'd catch my parachute trapeze and slide off the bar and pull the parachute out of a sack. I'd drop about 60 feet and the parachute 'll [*sic*] open."[32] Baldwin eventually claimed that he had made an astonishing 2,800 parachute jumps.[33]

Thomas Baldwin, when he was associated with the showman Park Van Tassel at California's Golden Gate Park in San Francisco, charged a spectator a dollar to go up in a tethered balloon to view the city. Later, when Tom Baldwin had a near monopoly in performing the parachute drop as part of the Van Tassel show, he traveled the United States and charged "$1500 a jump, or $1 a foot, or 50 percent of the gate."[34] Thus, the parachute act proved profitable in the 1880s.

Even before the 1889 arrival of William Ivy at Quincy, Illinois, the Baldwin brothers considered taking their exhibitions overseas to Europe and Asia. Reports of the foreign successes of other aeronauts circulated among various groups. Tom Baldwin's 1887 jumps in Quincy, where he received a $450 bonus and gold medal, and later on the East Coast, prompted G.A. Farina in London to extend an invitation for a British tour. Tom accepted the offer, and he and his wife arrived in the summer of 1888. He completed more than a dozen drops over London's Alexander Palace between July 28 and September 14, 1888. Thousands observed Baldwin's acts, including members of the royal family.[35]

A 1903 book stated, "Professor Baldwin [Thomas Baldwin], as he was termed, an American aeronaut, arrived in England in the summer of 1888, and commenced giving a series of exhibitions from the Alexander Palace with a parachute of his own invention." In London, the Baldwin balloon was judged to be somewhat small at nineteen feet in diameter, but the parachute was "reckoned to give safe descent to 250 lbs, which would include weight of man and apparatus."[36]

After the highly successful British tour, Tom Baldwin returned to Quincy with his earnings and a gold medal from the Balloon Society of Great Britain. It was then an appropriate time to bring William Ivy into the Baldwin ballooning and parachute acts.[37]

A number of events converged in 1889 with the inclusion of Ivy Baldwin in the Baldwin Brothers show. First, the twenty-three-year-old Ivy had progressed from his early circus days on a trapeze to an experienced and skillful showman with abilities ranging from tightrope walker to balloon parachutist. He had demonstrated the essential qualities of a true showman—the nerve or courage to try new, daring acts and the ability to learn quickly despite the lack of real schooling and training. Also, his life of moving about and the absence of meaningful roots made him readily available to an organization such as the Baldwin Brothers troupe. He was prepared to become a professional aeronaut.

Second, coincidental with Ivy's availability was the Baldwin brothers' need for an additional performer. Tom Baldwin had already established a notable reputation as a professional aeronaut, but his weight gain and his expansionist vision for his show led to a search for a new recruit. William Ivy admirably filled that requirement. The new man, Ivy Baldwin, could step into show performances immediately. Tom Baldwin had already experienced an overseas tour in Great Britain, and with the inclusion of Ivy Baldwin, he could turn his attention to other worldwide engagements.

Ivy Baldwin's association with the Baldwin Brothers show firmly established his role as a professional aeronaut. With the Baldwins, he would further hone his many aerial skills, and he would learn from Tom Baldwin how to promote his acts. Ivy's path to a career as an aerial entertainer and showman became ever clearer.

2

TOURING BEYOND THE UNITED STATES

Professor Ivy Baldwin would perform a balloon ascension at 4 p.m. in a central position in the lake, when he will fall with his parachute in the water.
—Anglo-American, *Mexico City, 1892*

In 1890, while Tom Baldwin weighed the possibility of touring outside the United States, he needed to fulfill other nationwide engagements. A notable one occurred at the opening of John Elitch's Zoological Gardens in Denver, Colorado, in May.

Denver's Elitch's Gardens started as a humble picnic area in a former apple orchard bordered by cottonwood trees. Mary and John Elitch soon added animals, creating a private zoo. They began enhancing the park by adding flowering gardens and a vaudeville stage. By May 1890, with sixteen acres, the Elitches were ready to celebrate a grand opening of a truly impressive amusement park. Invited guests included the premier showman P.T. Barnum and Mr. and Mrs. Tom Thumb. A musical vaudeville show would be the main entertainment.[38] To make the event more significant, the Baldwin brothers had been engaged to provide spectacular balloon ascensions and parachute drops. One report stated that the Baldwins earned $500 for each performance.[39]

Denver's *Rocky Mountain News* reported on May 22 that "the balloon ascension and parachute descension yesterday by Professor Baldwin attracted a large number of visitors, the event proving thrillingly successful in every way."[40] With the draw of large crowds, Elitch extended the performances of Tom and Ivy Baldwin, and on Memorial Day, one newspaper declared, "One of the greatest crowds that has yet visited the Zoo [Elitch's Gardens] witnessed the balloon ascension of Tom Baldwin yesterday at 4 o'clock."[41]

For Ivy, performances at Elitch's proved more significant than usual, as they introduced him to the Rocky Mountain city of Denver. After several subsequent years of touring shows in Asia and Mexico, Ivy Baldwin would return to Colorado and eventually make Denver his home.[42]

After the Denver and other western city stops, the Baldwin show moved westward and departed San Francisco for the Far East on the SS *City of Peking* on November 1, 1890. Tom, Sam and Ivy experienced nearly hurricane-level winds on their Pacific crossing but finally landed at Nagasaki, Japan, on November 21. They hurriedly made their way to Tokyo the following day. They soon discovered that another showman, Percival Spencer, had preceded them and was entertaining the Japanese with balloon ascensions.[43]

Not at all intimidated by competition from performances by another aeronaut, the Baldwin show began its balloon ascensions at Tokyo's Uyeno Park in December 1890. In contrast to their predecessor's ascensions, the Baldwins spiced up the program with an opening by a daring Ivy Baldwin leap from a 120- or 150-foot tower into a net.[44]

This was not the first time Ivy Baldwin had done a tower dive, but the exact beginning of Ivy's tower performances remains obscure. At some point, he added this dramatic stunt to his repertoire. Denver's amusement park crowds had watched some leaps, and they considered them "astonishing feats." One impressed newspaper reporter remarked that an air of excitement occurred at the beginning of Ivy's act:

> *The top of the tower seems to swing back and forth as the spectators look at it, and many persons present felt premonitions that something dreadful was about to happen. Baldwin always appears the least concerned person in the assemblage. Climbing to the top of the tower, he crawls out on a horizontal ladder, hooks his legs over the last rung and hangs head downward. Grasping a rope he slowly lets himself down until his toes catch. A shudder passes through the crowd and many people turn their eyes from the sight. Baldwin waves his hand, a small boy shouts and down goes a human form, gradually assuming a horizontal position as it approaches the ground. Baldwin strikes in the net squarely on his back and the next instant swings himself to the ground.*[45]

Ivy Baldwin (*left*) flight checks the balloon basket just before an Elitch's Gardens performance in Denver, Colorado. *History Colorado Collection.*

In another interview, Ivy was asked how he did his tower jumps without hurting himself. He replied, "I don't know. I did it right along. I started at a low height and kept getting higher all the time when I got to 120 feet I thought that was high enough."[46]

When asked what kind of sensation he experienced when in a tower dive, Ivy said, "O, very pleasant, indeed. It seems an instant, although I have had the drop timed and it requires three or four seconds to make the trip. I guide myself entirely with my head. On leaving the bar I hold my body perfectly rigid and as I descend I allow my legs to fall back just a little. It is a gradual turn all the way. I generally manage to strike the net squarely on my back. I have never been badly hurt on making the drop."[47]

Ivy used the rungs of a small ladder, positioned perpendicular to the tower's top, to get distance from the tower itself. Then he would release for his dive into a net. His aim was for the center of a net placed a mere 10 feet from the ground. Ivy said the net stretched from 8 feet wide and 40 feet long, meaning that from a view at 120 feet, it was indeed a very small target.[48]

In Tokyo, the Baldwins, always enterprising, hired locals to construct the Baldwin towers of flimsy-looking bamboo sections tied with fiber rope, which made the structure amazingly strong and solid. Tom and Ivy used guywires to provide additional stability. Even then, the tower looked rickety and strikingly precarious.

Ivy's tower performances especially appealed to Asian audiences. Spectators gasped when he climbed to the top of the tower and out on the tiny ladder. Even more excitement developed at a Tokyo performance when the Japanese expected to see a drop from a 150-foot tower. Some confusion had occurred as to whether Ivy would leap from 120 or 150 feet. Later, Ivy declared, "I advertised 150 feet. And the Japs wouldn't have it that way [a lesser height of 120 feet]. I had to do 150. I did it, but only once. I didn't advertise it any more."[49] Ivy's leap from a 150-foot tower seemed to create an unusual nervousness for him. He said, "I shut my eyes before I took the plunge." When he hit the net, he feared he had injured himself, particularly in his neck area. "I thought I was telescoped," he admitted.[50]

The Baldwins' exhibition, highlighted by Ivy's dramatic tower stunt, proved tremendously popular, attracting huge crowds. Even the Japanese emperor was impressed. He ordered his own artisans to prepare a silk kimono embroidered with a depiction of Ivy's tower leap and further decorated it with balloons and parachutes. In a subsequent interview, the emperor presented the kimono to Ivy, and it became one of Ivy's most cherished possessions.[51]

A balloon ascension usually followed Ivy's tower jump. Even balloon inflation fascinated the Japanese. An account at the time noted that in contrast to the Spencer silk balloon, the Baldwins' balloon was a big and grimy affair, made of red and white strips of coarse, strong cotton sewn together. Also, differing from the Spencer gas balloon, the Baldwins used a hot-air balloon. One report said, "The Baldwins had provided themselves, apparently, with nothing more than a pile of fire-wood and a can of kerosene." The journalist further remarked, "In short, it is impossible to conceive anything rougher than their whole system." A large wood fire soon got the hot air flowing to inflate the balloon, though. After approximately fifteen minutes, one of the Baldwins would quickly rise upward. Tom or Ivy would dangle at the end of a fifty-foot rope, do a few acts on the trapeze and then eventually parachute earthward from either the trapeze or the balloon basket.[52]

The Baldwins visited other large Japanese cities and then traveled to China, where they had performances in Shanghai and Hong Kong. Proceeding westward by steamship, they stopped in Saigon, Rangoon, Singapore, three towns in Java and at Calcutta and Madras in India. They eliminated Vladivostok, Russia, as a destination because agents there demanded an exorbitant share of profits.[53]

Ivy told a story of when he was performing in Java in one of his parachute acts and he happened to come down in some trees populated with hundreds of monkeys. Ivy said, "Yes, I came down in the woods there where they were at and the trees were just full of them. They were little, not very big monks, you know. But they're awful scary and they just scream." Ivy Baldwin always remembered the sound of this startling event. "They run from me, but it was like a cyclone to hear the noise they made going through the trees and things."[54]

After this whirlwind touring, with such extensive traveling in relatively few months, Tom Baldwin canceled unfilled contracts and decided to return to the United States in late spring of 1891. Tom Baldwin's pregnant wife demanded that their first child be born in their Quincy home and not in Asia. Ivy Baldwin, however, did not return to the United States until September 1891.[55]

The *Quincy Daily Journal* reported on September 24, 1891, "Ivy Baldwin, whom Tom adopted as a brother and took with him to Japan, arrived in Quincy shortly after midnight and is being introduced to the many friends of the Baldwin brother today." When Tom Baldwin introduced Ivy to the Quincy public, he referred to him as "the Ivy" and bragged, "'The Ivy' is the wonder of the world—the most daring man in the profession....His equal can't be produced." The newspaper indicated that Ivy would be a Baldwin "guest" for several months and that the community would likely be able to judge his "caliber as an aeronaut."[56]

When Tom Baldwin returned to Quincy, he reconsidered his vagabond life with the Baldwin shows, especially now that he was a father. The Baldwins decided to buy a thirty-two-acre portion of a Quincy fairgrounds, which included a renovated hotel, grandstands, a racecourse, a baseball diamond and even a bowling alley. They advertised it as Baldwin Park. Ivy Baldwin often managed a saloon in the park while still doing his usual entertaining performances. Tom Baldwin continued to do balloon ascensions and build balloons but left the more daring stunts to Ivy. Sam Baldwin assumed overall Baldwin Park management. Although Tom Baldwin would schedule other occasional tours, Baldwin Park became and remained their headquarters.[57]

Winter always meant a downtime for the Baldwin Brothers and their shows; therefore, it was not surprising that they booked exhibitions in Mexico during those cold months. Ivy Baldwin spent a limited time in Quincy after the Asia tour before he and Tom Baldwin left for Mexico City. They quickly got involved in winter festivals being staged in the city.

Colorado's Daring Ivy Baldwin

A newspaper reported on February 12, 1892, that a "Mr. M.A. Jackson, the well-known journalist and late editor of this paper [*Anglo-American*], has accepted the position of manager to Professor Ivy Baldwin the aeronaut." The article indicated big Baldwin plans: "Mr. Jackson will accompany the latter gentleman on his proposed tour through the West Indies, Central and South America."[58] This bit of news revealed that Ivy had assumed greater importance in both performances and management.

In the same Mexico City newspaper on February 12, a poem titled "The Aeronaut" was dedicated to "Prof. Ivy Baldwin and his manager M.A. Jackson":

Who is the voyager of the air,
Who in mid-heaven doesn't scare,
And when he drops will raise your hair?
That's Baldwin.

Who through the pathless storm cloud hies
And wander where the cyclone sighs
Or rules so high he scrapes the skies?
That's Baldwin.

Who when ballooning doesn't suit,
And back to earth he wants to scoot
Comes sailing down per parachute?
That's Baldwin.

Who harnesses old Hydrogen,
And makes him wonder now and then
To find he's been caught in a pen?
That's Baldwin.

Who sails the breeze in far Japan,
And makes the artless Chinaman
Forget a while about fan-tan?
That's Baldwin.

Who tells you slyly that he thinks,
He'll teach our Ivy several kinks!
He's nice, but its too bad he drinks.
That's Jackson.[59]

Poetry, however, didn't inspire Ivy Baldwin. "I got no use for poetry," remarked Ivy. "Down in Mexico a girl got stuck on me and kept writing poetry like that. I couldn't make heads or tails of it."[60]

On February 22, a different Mexico City newspaper reported that several tests of a captive balloon, one with an empty basket, had been completed and adjudged safe by city engineers. Subsequently, Ivy and several gentlemen "made a successful ascension and had a most delightful bird's eye view of the city below."[61]

Only a few days later, Mexico City newspapers reported on "The Great Event," a regatta on Lake Texcoco featuring some foreign crews and an Ivy Baldwin balloon ascension. Trying to heighten anticipation and, no doubt, attendance, one news source said, "Tomorrow will chronicle one of the greatest events of the Mexican boating world that has ever transpired in the vicinity of this capital." After the regatta, the paper printed, "Professor Ivy Baldwin would perform a balloon ascension at 4 p.m. in a central position in the lake, where he will fall with his parachute in the water." The newspapers expected fifteen thousand people to be in attendance.[62]

Mexico City newspapers did indicate that Ivy performed a few tower jumps in that country, but Ivy did not mention them nor did the papers give them much attention. Perhaps the Baldwins were so successful with the balloon attractions that they didn't see the need for the dangerous tower plunges. There was a hint of another reason: opposition by civic officials. Ivy said, "I was denied the privilege of making the drop. I was giving exhibitions at the time in the City of Mexico. The authorities considered it a suicidal affair and would not listen to a word of my explanations."[63]

On April 18, 1892, Mexico City newspapers carried an account of "A Brilliant Success Scored by Prof. Ivy Baldwin." Reports said that he had made a morning and afternoon ascension at the Castaneda gardens, a "popular suburban retreat, the Coney Island of Mexico." In the morning, "the weather was most favorable and the balloon ascended rapidly... where it encountered a current of wind which carried it in a circle around San Angel. Prof. Baldwin cut loose at a height of three fourths of a mile and gracefully sailed to terra firma." The afternoon ascension was even more noteworthy, according to the papers: "The weather in the early part of the afternoon was windy and cloudy, and Prof. Baldwin felt very much discouraged, but about four o'clock a few drops of rain fell and calmed the atmosphere so that Mr. Baldwin was able to inflate the balloon and make the most successful ascent of the season. He rose to the height of over a mile, and was fully three minutes in dropping to earth. On landing he was roundly cheered by the large concourse of people present."[64]

On the same day as the laudatory story of Ivy's balloon ascension, April 18, an *Anglo-American* reporter recorded some interesting comments from Ivy Baldwin. Ivy stated that his average balloon was 150 feet in circumference and 75 feet in height, requiring eight hundred or more yards of cloth. He used a hoop the size of a wagon wheel to keep the balloon mouth open. Ivy declared, "However much romance there may appear in ballooning, it is nothing less than a trade, and a difficult one, requiring long years of training and experience for its mastery." He continued, "In the first place it differs from other occupations in its constant excitement. To the aeronaut each ascent means fresh danger, and it is on this account, perhaps, that comparatively few engage in it." Ivy believed few people who observed a balloon ascension could understand or describe its accompanying sensations. "The aeronaut lives a lifetime in a few moments on his voyage," asserted Ivy.[65]

As might be expected, not all Ivy Baldwin balloon ascensions went well. On May 17, 1892, Mexican newspapers reported, "Prof. Ivy Baldwin made another most excellent balloon ascension from the Tivoli Ermita, at Tizapan on Sunday last…but his landing into a lava bed was nearly a fatal disaster. Ivy's balloon caught by a current of air drifted over orchards but then over the lava beds." When nearly a mile high, observing that there was no possibility of his sailing in his aircraft to a point beyond the vitreous substance, he cut himself loose and at a rate of nine hundred feet a minute started for earth, his parachute swaying in a most dangerous manner. Ivy couldn't escape a hard landing on "the irregular masses of volcanic rock," and he "bruised his head and hand and cut gashes in his feet, knees and elbows."[66]

A few days later, at Professor Ivy Baldwin's farewell ascension at Castaneda gardens, newspapers observed that although he had made another successful ascension and "turned his parachute loose," Ivy did not perform gymnastic feats on his trapeze, "as he was too lame and stiff to do so."[67]

Another memorable parachute act that occurred in Mexico resulted in the "cactus landing." Ivy claimed this painful incident occurred at San Luis Potosi. "I made a balloon ascension from the bull pen where they had bullfights," Ivy said. "I drifted right over San Luis and I was right over a cactus field but I didn't know it was cactus. I cut loose and I came down and came down right among those cactus. My back was full of 'em. I had purt [*sic*] near all night with a Mexican melting cattle grease on my back, scraped it off with a case knife to get the thorns out of my back."[68]

The hurting Ivy Baldwin completed his many exhibitions in Mexico City in late May. A paper that followed his exploits stated, "The Professor leaves tonight for his home in Quincy, Illinois, carrying with him best wishes of a host of friends."[69]

The Mexico exhibitions in the early months of 1892 must have been quite successful. The Baldwins had extended their stay in the country to May, inching into the time normally devoted to getting ready for the summer performances in the United States.

When the Baldwins finally gathered in Quincy, Tom and Ivy began manufacturing a new balloon. It would be called MARS, and the Quincy newspaper at the time declared, "It is the handsomest and best proportioned aerial monster that was ever constructed." The new balloon had a circumference of 114 feet and a height of 57 feet. The newspaper stated, "The material used in its construction is a French weave in which silk, linen and cotton are blended to give it the needed qualities of tenacity, pliability and lightness." The balloon had a trial inflation and then had its first coat of varnish applied. When five more coats of varnish were added, the MARS was expected to hold 25,000 cubic feet of gas. The balloon had a distinctive white color so that when it was inflated "it looked like a gigantic soap bubble," the *Quincy Daily Herald* asserted.[70] Ivy Baldwin, no doubt, watched and participated in the building of balloons while he was with the Baldwin shows and at the Quincy headquarters. He would put this balloon-building knowledge to use in the future.

Approximately ten thousand people attended the 1892 July 4 celebration at Baldwin Park in Quincy. The featured event was "Ivy Baldwin's soul-harrowing dive from a 100-foot tower." The *Quincy Daily Herald* declared, "This terrible jump was cheered fondly as the crowd witnessed its successful accomplishment."[71]

In the fall of 1892, Ivy Baldwin and the new MARS balloon had a notable event that attracted considerable attention. Ivy and a Quincy reporter, Eugene Brown, made a twilight ascension and a night trip of approximately ninety-two miles from Baldwin Park, landing in Briggsville. The *Chicago Times* noted that the "Daring Night Voyage" rose into the heavens "Four Miles from Earth," where "Villages Twinkled Like Stars in the Firmament."[72] After the successful night trip and landing, Ivy was reported to have said, "After all there's only one way to travel, and that is in a balloon."[73]

The success of the first Mexico tour in early 1892 prompted a second one the following year. On January 3, 1893, a Mexico City newspaper told about Ivy Baldwin's sixth ascension in the capital. The paper reported,

"The spectators out to view Prof. Baldwin's sixth ascension at the Castaneda Sunday afternoon were more numerous than on Christmas Day and they had the satisfaction of seeing a monster aerostat inflated with hot air in the teeth of a powerful wind and a slight drizzly rain—an occurrence singularly rare in ballooning." The headline for the news item stated, "Baldwin Defies the Elements and Sails Aloft."[74] This pointed to a long-term Ivy Baldwin principle—avoid canceling a performance whenever possible. As a consequence, some Ivy Baldwin balloon ascensions were borderline regarding safety.

A Baldwin balloon ascension on a late January 1893 Sunday proved special for a number of reasons. First, newspaper reports indicated that a gas balloon, rather than a hot-air one, had been used. The paper stated:

> *The balloon ascension last Sunday, at the Tivoli San Cosmo, proved to a large crowd of spectators that Baldwin Bros. are eminently practical in their line of business. The work of inflating the air ship was commenced early but owing to the fact of the large generating tank being defective considerable delay was experienced and the "first charge" did not get in working order until about 11 o'clock when the tank was again quickly recharged.... The spectators commenced to arrive on the grounds and they then saw the balloon partially filled and a large, steady stream of gas flowing through a hose into it from a cooling tub. The aerostat was at this hour tugging at the sand bags surrounding it and two hours later it was in readiness for the voyage.*

The news account also revealed that Tom Baldwin had been supervising the filling of the balloon.[75]

A second event associated with the Tivoli ascension called attention to how a balloon could be a vehicle for advertising. The paper elaborated, "A large number of English speaking gentlemen were holding the ropes as Mr. Fadrique Lopez, an editor of the *Universal*, and Prof. Ivy Baldwin took their places in the car to exclamations of joy from the vast throng gathered on the grounds to see the ascension." After the balloon was released and rose higher and higher, editor "Lopez unfurled a banner over the American and Mexican flags on the basket, on which was printed: 'Read the Universal, the leading journal in Mexico.'" Not only was the banner advertisement on the balloon basket, but Mr. Lopez, from time to time, also began "throwing out advertising matter that found its way to hundreds of streets in the capital and to roof tops, where people had gathered in thousands to see the ascension."[76] While this was not the first balloon used in advertising, it did graphically confirm it as an example of a revenue source from any advertising-minded client.

Another interesting revelation in this one ascension was the news that Ivy Baldwin could be audacious, if not foolhardy, in another way: "When at great attitude Prof. Ivy Baldwin was seen to climb below the basket on a rope and smoke a cigarette, a most daring feat which caused untold amazement to the tens of thousands who were watching the balloon."[77] Ivy had smoked from precarious positions below a balloon before, but clearly, the newspaper reporter and the ground observers were aware that smoking and flying in a hydrogen gas balloon risked a horrible explosion.

Ivy told a story in later years emphasizing again the dangers involved in flying hydrogen-filled balloons. The incident, Ivy said, nearly shattered his supreme confidence in anticipating every possible contingency:

> *Once I felt my last hour had come. I was making a series of ascensions in the City of Mexico and was getting along swimmingly, when one day an unexpected danger was presented. The Mexicans have a way of their own in which to celebrate their Fourth of July. I was not read up on Mexican customs and did not know that they were especially fond of fire balloons as a means of exhibiting their patriotism. I was floating over the beautiful valley, taking in some of the most lovely scenery in the world when several bright objects appeared coming toward the balloon. I found to my dismay that the objects were fire balloons and several of them were aiming at the big affair which carried me along. If I had been provided with a parachute I might have cut loose even at the risk of being drowned in the lake but all I could do was to throw out ballast and reach the greatest height possible. It was for some time a race for life but the balloon responded as the load was lightened and the fire balloons passed out of sight.*[78]

This event reflected Ivy Baldwin's balloon piloting skills and his great confidence in his abilities.

During this same exhibition season, spectators nervously watched Ivy Baldwin experience a desperate time in flight when he became entangled in some ropes and his parachute harness. He ended up cutting himself loose from the balloon but, according to reports, shot toward earth with unprecedented speed.

Another January 1893 newspaper account told about "Prof. Ivy Baldwin" taking a bride and groom on an ascension following their wedding. After

Ivy had inflated his balloon, the bride, "in her bridal robes and veil, was assisted into the basket," followed by the groom and Ivy. The balloon "shot straight into the air to the height of 5,000 feet," where an air current caught it and they traveled some four miles. The landing ended well, and Ivy joined celebrators in raising glasses of champagne. The conclusion of the article said, "The Baldwin Brothers leave for the United States…remaining a few days at Laredo to give an exhibition."[79]

The *Quincy Daily Whig*, in its February 15, 1893 edition, headlined an article declaring, "Gratifying Success of Tom and Ivy Baldwin the City of Mexico—Banqueted by Everybody from President Díaz Down." The paper added, "They went to the City of Mexico under contract a couple of months ago to give a series of aeronautic exhibitions, and in that time have completed the conquest of Mexico. Their exhibitions have been invariably successful, and in all their ascensions they have not yet had a failure." The newspaper revealed that the contract in Mexico was $6,000 for three months work, with $500 every Saturday night. The paper viewed this as not only operationally successful but also a "profitable trip financially."[80]

An interesting note to the Baldwins' 1893 Mexico trip concerned their performances immediately following failure of an exhibition by a "couple of famous French aeronauts." It seemed that the French men had contracted to build a huge balloon to carry as many as thirty-two people. It proved so heavy that it could not rise and lift its own weight. The French failure did, by comparison, heighten the American successes.[81]

On April 18, 1893, the *Quincy Daily Herald* took note of the return of the Baldwins from their Mexico winter tour. The paper remarked that Tom and Ivy were "back in civilization again" and proclaimed them "kings" with loads of laurels. Both Tom and Ivy reportedly had numerous stories about their Mexican experiences.[82]

When Ivy reached Quincy in the spring of 1893, he found that parts of Baldwin Park had been leveled and the rest severely damaged by a tornado or tornado-type winds. The Baldwin Brothers did invest money and hard work restoring their headquarters, but the park had lost some of its previous luster.[83] In addition, balloon ascensions and parachute drops had declined in revenue. In his Mexico interview, Ivy had noted, "There is less profit in the business now than formerly; the novelty of the ordinary balloon ascension no longer exists for Americans."[84]

At Baldwin Park, however, the Baldwins sought to buttress their balloon revenues by securing more wedding party balloon ascensions. The idea of providing such events for courageous married couples had developed earlier in the United States and continued in Mexico. While they gained some additional income, taking up a bride and groom would be sporadic at best. When Ivy finally returned to Quincy, he continued Baldwin show performances, including a notable wedding event on July 4. According to the *Quincy Daily Herald*, bad weather plagued the scheduled celebration, and "the large balloon 'City of Burlington,' after having been filled and conveyed to the park burst and all the gas escaped." A backup balloon was brought to the park, and "the bride and groom, safely united by Judge McDonnel, took their places in the car immediately and were wafted to the clouds by Ivy Baldwin." After reaching a height of two miles, it drifted eight miles northeast before landing. The bride and groom then returned to the city and were greeted with cheers.[85]

Another significant milestone occurred in Ivy's life at this same time. He married Bertha Louise Sherman, who, born in 1867, was a year younger than Ivy.[86] This union took place in Quincy. With a new bride, Ivy began weighing his future more seriously, perhaps contemplating a place to settle. Interestingly, there is no record that Ivy Baldwin and his new wife tried a marriage balloon ascension.

At this time, in the summer of 1893, several events led Ivy Baldwin to terminate his partnership with the Quincy-based Baldwin Brothers. First, a decline in profitability of balloon ascensions and related aerial acts had developed, portending a bleaker future for the balloon show business. The Baldwin partnership had been good for Tom and Sam Baldwin and for Ivy, but the slowdown in show business called for a reassessment of future prospects. There was no indication of any friction between the Baldwins, and Ivy's separation was apparently an amicable one. It is likely that the more mature Ivy thought that he could profit from his single exhibitions. There was another factor in Ivy's decision to leave the Baldwin enterprise. He now had a new wife and a greater responsibility that had to be weighed. He probably had thoughts of establishing his own home base and eyed the West as a more lucrative place for his future performances. He fondly remembered the Elitch's Gardens exhibitions, so he decided to return to Denver.

On August 9, 1893, the *Colorado Evening Sun* noted, "Balloonist Baldwin, the Well-known Aeronaut, Arrives for a Stay in Denver."[87]

Denver's beautiful, now well-established Elitch's Gardens warmly welcomed Ivy Baldwin. He had no trouble resuming his various acts, as his previous performances at Elitch's inaugural had attracted large crowds. However, Ivy remained in Denver for only a few weeks, as he then journeyed to Stockton, California. He participated in some festival shows in California.

Colorado's Daring Ivy Baldwin

On September 8, 1893, the *Stockton Evening Mail* reported on an Ivy Baldwin disaster as a near fatal incident. According to the newspaper, Ivy's balloon "Bursts and Falls" in mid-air. The article began, "Ivy Baldwin, the aeronaut, in making a balloon ascension yesterday at Goodwater Grove narrowly escaped being killed. Had it not been for his remarkable presence of mind and his wonderful agility in going from the trapeze to loose the parachute, in less time than it can be told, he would now be a corpse."[88] Ivy Baldwin had barely survived another life-threatening mishap, but he was not about to cancel his performances.

The undaunted Ivy Baldwin had another balloon made at Stockton and rapidly returned to his ascensions and stunts. Another Stockton newspaper described a later performance this way:

> *The balloon ascension by Ivy Baldwin at Goodwater grove on Sunday last was a great success. The new balloon, manufactured at great expense for the occasion, was never equaled in this city. The crowd that collected at the grove was the largest that ever gathered there and they showed their appreciation of the show by enthusiastic applause. The tight-rope walk in the evening by the same performer, Ivy Baldwin, was not only a great success but was wonderful. His feats caused beholders to hold their breath, though they were done with such ease and grace as showed the long experience had given him perfect skill in the balancing art.*[89]

At the same time as Ivy's Stockton shows, he added a new wrinkle, a cloud swing, to his balloon ascensions. One reporter described the new stunt: "Attached to the balloon is the parachute and to the latter a rope a hundred feet long at the end of which is a ring. Into this ring the daring aeronaut places one foot, catches the rope with one hand and ascends with the balloon swinging like a human pendulum. When in the act he feels enough he clambers up to the parachute, cuts it loose and down he comes."[90]

Ivy, improvising once again, found a way to inject a new twist into a performance. He realized that even the most spectacular stunts could become stale. Something new was needed to hold and attract the crowds.

Instead of returning to Denver after the Stockton engagement, Ivy apparently remained in California to do other exhibitions. In February 1894, he was in San Francisco offering performances as part of that city's Midwinter Exposition. The *San Francisco Chronicle*, on February 3, reported on "Ivy Baldwin's Sensational Flight" from a tower. The newspaper stated, "A fall of 150 feet whether into water, a net, or any other contrivance,

Ivy Baldwin (*center*) inspects his balloon as it inflates at Denver's Elitch's Gardens amusement park. *History Colorado Collection.*

ordinarily means certain death to the individual making the drop. But there is in San Francisco at present a modest and unassuming little gentleman, who not only 'took a tumble' to the tune of 150 feet but is going to do it again, if not several times at the Midwinter Exposition grounds. This gentleman is Ivy Baldwin of the celebrated Baldwin family of aeronauts and daring gymnasts."[91]

The San Francisco newspaper went on to describe Ivy's tower drop and included a sketch to illustrate the feat. The story claimed, "The people of but two American cities have had the pleasure of witnessing Mr. Baldwin's marvelous leap, those of Denver and Quincy, Ill. Baldwin has given most of his exhibitions in Europe and Asia and but [*sic*] recently returned to this country." To generate further interest, the report stated, "A gentleman who witnessed one of Ivy Baldwin's sensational drops in Denver, said the other day that it was the most astonishing feat of daring he had ever looked at."[92]

Ivy Baldwin did make his way back to Denver in time for that city's 1894 summer amusement park openings. The California exhibitions had kept him employed during the winter months. Although he must have had ideas of taking up permanent residence in Denver, he evidently harbored dreams of future shows, even tours overseas. A news report said Ivy had written to a Quincy friend saying, "He is preparing to make another trip to Japan believing there will be big money in it for him."[93] Further into the months of 1894, however, Ivy Baldwin must have reconsidered foreign touring plans. Looming in his future was an entirely different experience—a truly surprising turn in his aeronaut career.

3
MILITARY BALLOONIST

The Aeronaut Who Is Known to Many Thousands of People World Over Will Put His Knowledge of Ballooning to Practical Use in the Interests of Uncle Sam.
—Daily News, *Denver, 1894*

Warmer temperatures in the spring of 1894 led to the gradual openings of Denver's amusement parks. After his winter performances in California, Ivy Baldwin eagerly welcomed Colorado exhibition opportunities, the most prominent being Elitch's Gardens in Denver. Ivy began his remarkable tower dives and, more frequently, the balloon ascensions with associated aerial acrobatics. His acts continued to attract large crowds.

One of the most notable summer balloon ascensions occurred in early August 1894. Denver's *Daily News* arranged for a "Pictures from the Sky" photographic expedition with Ivy Baldwin. A new balloon, the City of Denver, was to be piloted by Ivy while attempting to use new photographic technology to obtain pictures of the city. The newspaper stated, "The lenses carried will permit successful results at almost any range, being of several different focal lengths. One of the new lenses, lately introduced to photography, and called a tele-photo lens, will be taken along to use on distant views." As was typical of the state-of-the-art at the time, there was concern about the fragile and sensitive plates. "The plates will be of the most rapid orthochromatic variety made and are of special emulsions adapted for long distance photography. All that is necessary for successful results will depend on the weather and

Noted Denver photographer Harry A. Buckwalter stands in the Ivy Baldwin balloon basket before his sensational, accidental solo flight in 1894. *Harry A. Buckwalter Collection, History Colorado.*

coming down easily and in proper shape. For work of this nature glass plates only can be used and they will not allow very rough handling, although every precaution will be taken for their preservation."[94]

The sponsoring newspaper for this scientific balloon trip expressed great confidence in Ivy Baldwin, despite the concerns about the photographic plates. "Ivy Baldwin, the aeronaut of the trip, needs no introduction to anybody. For years past he has made ascensions in every part of the world and is recognized as one of the best men in his line living. He has made many trips in the air from Elitch's gardens and always without hitch or accident. When he undertakes to make *The News'* expedition next Sunday a success it is almost an assured fact, barring only the weather."[95]

Despite the trust in the piloting skills of Ivy Baldwin, a remarkable turn of events produced a most dramatic August 12 balloon voyage. First, trouble gassing the balloon caused delays in launching. The initial gas inflation did not produce much lift, so the balloon was switched to another gas generator.

"A trial of the pulling power was again made and the balloon lifted Mr. Baldwin, *The News* reporter and two bags of ballast." On the way to Elitch's Gardens, however, the balloon brushed against trees and houses and the bag ripped. Holes had to be sewed and another lifting trial was made.[96]

As the balloon was made ready again, Ivy and a reporter for the *News*, Harry H. Buckwalter, a prominent Denver photographer and newspaper photojournalist, stood next to the basket. When the lines slackened, the balloon failed to rise. Then, according to Buckwalter, the following dialogue took place: "'Take out those cameras,' said Baldwin. The cameras and ballast were taken out and still no rise. 'Take off your coat,' again said Baldwin. The coat was taken off without any effect on the balloon. Then, in a discouraged tone, Baldwin said, 'Well, what'll we do?' 'Will you trust the balloon in my hands?' asked *The News* man. 'Certainly, if you'll risk the trip,' was the reply. 'All right, get out of the basket and give me the camera.'"

Amazingly, Baldwin got out and the camera and coat were handed in. Ivy issued a simple instruction: "Don't pull the valve cord until you strike. She won't lift over two miles and when she strikes you will probably get dragged a little, but that won't hurt you much."[97]

Several friends advised Buckwalter to back out. A small boy shouted, "Goodbye, mister; you're going to die this time" as the balloon lifted off. A rope trailed on the ground, threatening to entangle a woman and other onlookers. As the rope broke free, it hit an electric wire with the jolt, shaking the basket and breaking the thermometer. The balloon finally soared upward.

Buckwalter later described his emotions: "The sensation was that the earth was falling away from the balloon which seemed not to move." He said, "The view of the gardens was grand, but a photograph was out of the question on account of pulling up the long anchor rope which took approximately five minutes."[98]

Shortly after five o'clock in the evening, the balloon aneroid showed eleven thousand feet or about six thousand feet above Denver. During a moment of relief, Buckwalter took a few photographs and declared, "The view was getting grander every moment." The balloon slowly revolved and drifted northwesterly toward the smelters and Jesuit college. Thirty minutes later, the balloon's rise stopped, and a slight noise at the top revealed the disconcerting fact that the balloon was starting down. Buckwalter thought he could see daylight at the top and realized that gas was escaping. Buckwalter believed a rip had occurred at the top, but after the flight, Ivy determined that a tear had not occurred but that Buckwalter had accidentally pulled open the valve.

A current of air pushed the balloon northward, toward the Westminster University building. About a quarter of a mile beyond the university building, the basket struck the ground. Buckwalter was knocked off his feet but could not get out of the basket because he was entangled in some rigging.[99]

Buckwalter tried pulling the valve cord to release all of the gas, but it seemed stuck. The balloon basket then bounced from the ground one hundred feet in the air. Buckwalter got the anchor rope out, and after several more bounces, the anchor caught and then slipped, dragging Buckwalter and the basket through cacti for three-quarters of a mile. Camera and photo paraphernalia fell across the fields. The basket appeared to be headed for a barbed wire fence with short posts. Buckwalter jumped from the basket, and the balloon shot up again and drifted away to near Henderson, fourteen miles from Denver, before finally coming down to a complete stop.[100]

Surprisingly, Buckwalter was not seriously hurt, but he needed help in another way. "A nearby resident came up to him and seeing the amount of cactus needles sticking out of the body of the amateur balloonist, he smiled and offered to play surgeon. It was necessary to get behind the carriage and partly undress to get at the worst damage. But soon the big needles were removed and the whole party drove back to Mr. Whitely's house. Here plenty of witch hazel and a spare handkerchief soon fixed matters up."[101]

Only one of Buckwalter's plates survived. The great scientific balloon flight had failed. From the very earliest days of balloons, there had been interest in similar experiments because the balloon enabled passengers to observe objects from a great height. Furthermore, aerial photography, as in Buckwalter's case, could provide a means of documenting balloon observations. Buckwalter was not the first person to tackle aerial photography. In the latter half of the nineteenth century, a Parisian portrait photographer and balloonist known as Nadar was credited as the first person to take and develop aerial photographs. No one, however, could have dreamed at that time that Buckwalter's aerial photography eventually would lead to precise photo images from the realm of space.

Everyone was relieved that Buckwalter, although enduring cactus needles, had escaped death. His harrowing experience would not deter him from making future balloon ascensions, and he actually garnered additional fame as a true adventurer.

Ivy Baldwin, with the assistance of men on horseback, retrieved much of his damaged balloon. As a small point, perhaps, he could again claim that he had not canceled an ascension. However, he reportedly said afterward that he henceforth would do his own hydrogen gas generation. But a big question lingered: what prompted Ivy Baldwin to take the immense risk of allowing an unskilled newspaper photographer to pilot a balloon? An answer to that question never materialized.

On September 17, the *Daily News* published an article noting that Denver's amusement park season was nearing an end. The headline declared, "Everybody Taking Advantage of Present Opportunity—Balloon Wedding Yesterday."[102] This balloon wedding may have been Ivy's final act for the 1894 summer season.

While Denver's amusement park season may have closed quietly, sudden and shocking news appeared about Ivy Baldwin's future. The *Daily News* ran a large headline on November 12, 1894, announcing, "Ivy Baldwin Joins the United States Army." A secondary headline declared, "The Aeronaut Who Is Known to Many Thousands of People World Over Will Put His Knowledge of Ballooning to Practical Use in the Interests of Uncle Sam."[103] No doubt, this news came as a surprise to many Denver residents and others scattered throughout the United States, such as in Quincy, Illinois, home base for the Baldwin shows. There had been no hint that Ivy would abruptly become a military balloonist. The many fans of daredevil Ivy Baldwin and fellow aeronauts were undoubtedly stunned.

Apparently, the army's recruitment of Ivy had been underway for some months. Captain William A. Glassford, who commanded the Signal Corps balloon at nearby Fort Logan, became aware of Ivy's balloon ascensions at Elitch's and elsewhere. According to the Denver newspaper, "The vigilant eye of the chief of the signal corps observed in Baldwin a most promising aeronaut and several weeks ago Captain Glassford invited Baldwin to consider seriously a proposition to cast his fortunes with the signal corps."[104] Captain Glassford needed to secure the approval of Ivy's recruitment from his boss, Brigadier General Adolphus W. Greely, chief Signal Corps officer of the army, and the support of Major General Alexander M. McCook, commander of the Department of the Colorado in Denver. With the support of these key commanders, the army offered to make Ivy Baldwin a sergeant in the Signal Corps, backdated his enlistment to June 20, 1894, and, in effect, placed him in charge of Fort Logan's balloon ascensions under the general direction of Captain Glassford. A long-term goal was to use Ivy's knowledge and skills to strengthen the army's balloon service. Newspaper reports indicated that Ivy would construct a hydrogen gas plant and do tethered balloon ascents regularly.[105]

Ivy accepted the army's proposition, and after correspondence between Colorado and Washington, D.C., a telegram from the secretary of war on

November 10 placed Ivy Baldwin in the U.S. Army with duty at Fort Logan. "The nervy young man became a full fledged sergeant in the signal corps of the department of the Colorado last Saturday and will hereafter act under authority of Uncle Sam," proclaimed the news accounts.[106]

Ivy Baldwin's decision to become a military balloonist may have been triggered by several events. Like Tom Baldwin, his mentor, he had married and needed to consider establishing a stable home with less touring. Furthermore, his wife, Bertha, was pregnant with their first son, Ira W. Baldwin, who was born on January 8, 1895. At the same time, Denver's prospering amusement parks seemed to offer an ideal home base. His military duty would still allow him to be stationed in Denver. Also, as previously mentioned, the U.S. aeronaut performances were declining in profitability. Ivy's military opportunity offered a timely response to his needs while providing an intriguing challenge of strengthening the army's balloon corps. Certainly, Ivy would not gain economically with his sergeant's pay. Even a newspaper observed that Uncle Sam "may not be as liberal a paymaster as the general public."[107]

Ivy did not escape the usual physical when entering military service. A local newspaper stated that "Sergeant Baldwin is a bright young man, 28 years old, an athlete and a perfect example of physical manhood." The account added, "Huntington, medical director of the department [Department of the Colorado], pronounces Baldwin one of the most perfectly developed men he has ever examined."[108]

Sergeant Ivy Baldwin and Captain Glassford were to be key players in General Greely and General McCook's vision of the future for the balloon corps: "Under the practical instruction of Sergeant Baldwin, it is expected that the sergeants of the signal corps from all parts of the country will gain thorough knowledge of ballooning. At the same time, they will be instructed in long distance signaling. It is proposed to familiarize the army with practical ballooning by sending the balloons and steel storage tubes containing compressed hydrogen gas to different army posts." General McCook received credit for espousing the plan of "conveying the balloons to the posts."[109]

Captain Glassford and Sergeant Baldwin had additional plans in that they hoped to add another balloon at Fort Logan. Tom Baldwin and Ivy had started building balloons during the course of their exhibitions, and Ivy's balloon-building experience would be put to use. General McCook became a big supporter of this endeavor and urged an appropriation for this purpose. In January 1895, the general was quoted as desiring to see a new war balloon before he retired: "Plans have been made by which the air ship can be built in Denver at a cost of about one-third of that required in the manufacture of the 'General Myer' [Fort Logan's balloon at the time] in France. Captain Glassford estimates that with the assistance of Sergeant Baldwin he can turn out the balloon complete for $700. No such balloon as is contemplated has ever been made on this side of the Atlantic and the process will be watched with great interest by aeronauts in all parts of the country."[110]

Having two war balloons, according to General McCook, would allow for more exhibitions at different army posts, giving signal men more experience with different elevations and circumstances.[111]

From the beginning of the Captain Glassford–Sergeant Baldwin team, a division of labor existed. Captain Glassford would emphasize balloon experimentation, while Ivy would handle balloon operations. One newspaper stated, "Captain Glassford furnishes the technical knowledge and Baldwin puts the plans into execution." Not surprisingly, "the nervy sergeant is perfectly willing to take a journey 4,000 or 5,000 feet toward the clouds providing Captain Glassford is scientifically satisfied that the machine is reasonably safe."[112]

The creation of the team, along with the support of Generals Greely and McCook, signaled a new era of balloon use in the Signal Corps of the U.S. Army. After the Civil War balloon operations by Thaddeus S.C. Lowe, head of the union balloon detachment, the army's balloon activities had virtually ended. This occurred despite Professor Lowe's notable success in demonstrating balloon reconnaissance in the fall of 1861, with a balloon named Washington. This success resulted in Quartermaster General M.C. Meigs authorizing construction of four new balloons and support equipment. A total of five balloons were thus available for Civil War combat use. A high point of Lowe's balloon service occurred during the Battle of Fair Oaks on May 31, 1862, when balloon observation led General George B. McClellan, commander of the Army of the Potomac, to move reinforcements to counter a Confederate attack. Despite somewhat limited achievements, the balloon corps completely disbanded in 1863, a victim of weather conditions, poor balloon administration and the contentious interplay of various personalities.[113]

A small army balloon revival began in 1891. From 1863 to the 1890s, the United States had no military balloons, although various countries, notably in Europe, had incorporated balloons in their armies. The U.S. Army's change began when Brigadier General Adolphus W. Greely secured an appropriation to start a balloon corps and established a Signal Corps balloon section in 1892. Greely, who had fought and was wounded as a private in the Civil War, had gained an officer's commission and held various assignments in the Signal Corps, particularly the weather service, leading to being named the chief Signal Corps officer in 1886. He had a six-month tour in Europe, where he became aware of the use of balloons during the Franco-Prussian War. When the weather service was separated from the Signal Corps and assigned to the Department of Agriculture in 1891, Greely turned to strengthening the military signaling mission and adding an aeronautical element. "The Chief Signal Officer has long appreciated the importance of balloons in active military operations," he stated.[114] With a vision far beyond most in the military at that time, Greely called on the attention of the secretary of war to show how the United States had fallen behind Europeans in military balloon operations and noted benefits he anticipated in aerial navigation. Also, he made it known that he favored the English use of captive skin balloons.[115]

General Greely sent Lieutenant William A. Glassford to Europe to further investigate European balloon developments and operations. Glassford had spent two years at the Naval Academy but had subsequently enlisted in the army, eventually obtaining a Signal Corps commission. He quickly became a noted meteorologist, with accolades for his accurate weather reporting. After arriving in Europe in July 1892, Glassford, following General Greely's orders, surveyed the status of European aeronautics for a year and then purchased a military balloon from the French balloon maker Lachambre. The balloon, constructed with goldbeater skin, was named General Myer in honor of the first chief Signal Corps officer, Dr. A.J. Myer. After being shipped to the United States, in the fall of 1893, the General Myer was sent to Chicago, where it was to be exhibited at Chicago's World Columbian Exposition. A crew from the Signal Corps School of Instruction at Fort Riley, Kansas, took charge of the exhibition.[116] Interestingly, Thomas Scott Baldwin was secured to do the first ascension. At the conclusion of the fair in October 1893, the General Myer was sent to Fort Riley and placed under the command of Lieutenant Joseph E. Maxfield, an 1881 Harvard graduate.[117]

Meanwhile, Captain Glassford received an assignment to be chief signal officer for General McCook and the Department of the Colorado in Denver in January 1894. McCook asked that the General Myer be assigned to his command, and in the fall of 1894, it was ordered to be shipped to Fort Logan. Glassford, by now a thoroughgoing balloon enthusiast, set about preparing wagons, hydrogen tanks and other generation and compression equipment to support the General Myer. It was at this time that Glassford sought to recruit Ivy Baldwin.[118]

At Fort Logan, Glassford and Baldwin assembled the gas support equipment, conducted ground-to-air communications, practiced balloon signaling and even experimented with aerial photography. Captain Glassford worked on a Code of Balloon Tactics that would be adopted by the army. A demonstration of these progressive steps occurred when Major General Nelson A. Miles, commander-in-chief of the U.S. Army, came to Fort Logan and watched a balloon drill. Sudden gusts of wind impacted any smooth handling of the General Myer, but the exhibition was considered a success. The next day, it was scheduled to photograph an enemy's position from the balloon. Reportedly, all of this activity would be "showing the world that the United States was not behind foreign armies in the matter of advanced ballooning."[119]

Unfortunately, on May 8, 1895, a serious accident occurred at Fort Logan when Ivy Baldwin barely escaped death and the General Myer actually escaped the fort.

A Denver newspaper reported on that day's event by first noting how many city visitors had come to the post to enjoy a spring outing. "The smiling springtime brought out hundreds of people from the city and every train heading to the post was crowded with sightseers," said the paper. In addition, there were bicycle parties and carriages, and "the visitors consisted largely of beautifully dressed ladies." The approximately one thousand assembled visitors then experienced a "sensation," with the Ivy Baldwin balloon ascension planned only to a height of the tethering cable. "The monster bag had been waddling about for hours, having been filled with gas from the tubes which were charged from the gas machine at the post. At 4 p.m. Baldwin shouted, 'Let 'er go!' and steadily the balloon mounted in the air."

Surprisingly, Ivy had considered the ascension an "experimental trip," and he had not attached the basket. Suddenly, a fierce gust sent the balloon and Ivy, hanging in the rigging, against the side of an officer row house. The tethering cable snagged in a roof gable, and the balloon began swinging back and forth, repeatedly throwing Ivy against the brick side of the structure. Appalled spectators could not offer assistance. Another sudden gust of wind thrust Ivy closer to the ground, where he made a great leap aided by a nearby spectator. In an instant, the cable broke and became free, and the balloon sailed away. Ivy survived with only serious bruises.[120] The newspaper applauded Ivy Baldwin's narrow escape and called him a fort hero.

The General Myer, speeding away, became a speck in the sky. Disgusted, Baldwin exclaimed, "I would have worked my way down all right" if he had managed to stay with the air bag. Shortly thereafter, Ivy jumped on a buckboard and started out in the direction of flight to recover the errant balloon. He successfully found the General Myer, but he discovered that its fragile goldbeater skin had been irreparably ripped apart. Thus the era of the General Myer had come to an end.[121]

A lack of Signal Corps funding seemed to doom a balloon replacement and the Fort Logan balloon detachment. Balloon advocate Glassford fervently appealed to the generals for money to construct another. Sergeant Baldwin, with his wife's support, offered to build a new balloon if some funding could be found to buy materials. Glassford, relying on Ivy Baldwin's estimates, succeeded in getting an appropriation of $700 for a pongee silk-type envelope.[122]

In the summer of 1895, Sergeant Ivy Baldwin and his wife, Bertha, started work on a new balloon at their residence on South Broadway in Denver. Mrs. Baldwin did the cutting and sewing. A newspaper reported that Mrs. Baldwin "takes a great deal of interest in her husband's profession, and is of great assistance to him."[123] Ivy constructed the rigging, and he planned to use the General Myer basket. The pongee silk received multiple layers of varnish to make it more airtight.[124] When completed during the 1896–97 winter, the resulting balloon had a fourteen-thousand-cubic-foot capacity, meaning it had a scaled-down ability to lift only one man and ballast. At about the same time, a large wooden hangar was authorized in fiscal year 1896, and construction began at Fort Logan to house the new balloon.[125]

Ivy Baldwin apparently had an understanding with the army when he enlisted so that he could continue participating in Denver amusement park balloon ascensions and perform various aerial acts. His exhibitions took place on weekends and holidays when, presumably, he had free time from Fort Logan duties. This privilege was highlighted in a nearly fatal accident toward the end of Elitch's Gardens' 1896 summer season. Denver's *Daily News* graphically described the Sunday, August 30 incident:

> *About 4:30 o'clock, in the south end of the gardens, the inflating of the huge silk balloon began. Baldwin and his assistant, a black man named Fred Frazier, took their position under the folds of the air ship, in order to see that the cloth filled in a proper manner, while Professor Darling, an aeronaut of Manhattan Beach, superintended the firing on the outside. A large crowd of people surrounded the balloon at the time and a dozen or more held it to the ground, ready for the signal from Baldwin for a release.*

The hydrogen-filled balloon that Ivy Baldwin and his wife, Bertha, fabricated rests in its balloon hangar at Fort Logan just before the Spanish-American War in 1898. *National Archives Photo.*

When the stately bag had filled with vapor, Baldwin emerged and clutching hold of the trapeze bar attached to the parachute, which hung from the balloon, shouted, "Let 'er go boys." The balloon soared skyward but immediately headed for some tall cottonwood trees, striking one of the largest, knocking Ivy from the trapeze and into the tree. Somewhat dazed, Ivy fell about 65 feet, with tree branches breaking his fall and probably preventing his death.[126]

A balloon ascension, with Ivy Baldwin standing above the basket, occurs in the winter near the Fort Logan balloon hangar. *National Archives Photo.*

Ivy Baldwin's injuries included a "contusion on the right side of his face, a broken arm, possible internal injuries, and several bruises of more or less importance."[127] He was hastily taken to St. Anthony's hospital by a police ambulance. Ivy's fall and obviously severe condition prompted several news sources to report he had been killed in the accident. In Ivy's hometown, Houston, Texas, a newspaper published an article headlined "Baldwin's Fatal Fall."[128] In Denver, an evening newspaper story likewise reported that Baldwin had been killed.[129]

Ivy, however, survived the crash into the tree and his extensive injuries, but this incident broke his self-claimed safety record of never having a serious injury during his many balloon ascensions.

After recuperating from his many physical problems, Ivy resumed his balloon duties at Fort Logan, working on a number of signal service experiments. Denver's *Daily News* reported on August 28, 1897, about an effort to test "night ballooning," with Ivy Baldwin providing two large balloons.[130] Over the next months, the Fort Logan Signal Corps detachment continued activities to refine balloon support equipment, such as the hydrogen gas wagons and generating equipment and handling procedures. Captain Glassford made it clear that he wanted military observers in the balloon basket and that he expected only tethered balloon operations at a safe distance from enemy shooters.[131]

Little did Sergeant Baldwin and Captain Glassford and all the Fort Logan personnel know that an actual war test would occur in only a few more months. During a period of approximately four years, the Baldwin-Glassford team had kept alive a small U.S. Army balloon corps. It would not have happened without the remarkable skills of Sergeant Ivy Baldwin.

4

OFF TO THE SPANISH-AMERICAN WAR

> *What do I think of the balloon in war? It is the coming ticket, and sure to be adopted by the government, the same as it has been by England, Germany and France.*
> —Quincy Morning Whig, *1898*

The 1898 annual report of the U.S. Army's Department of the Colorado stated that "instructing, both practical and theoretical, was given during the year [1897–98] to the signaling detachment at Fort Logan in generation of hydrogen gas, compression of the gas in storage tubes, inflation of the balloon, making ascensions and reeling in balloon from the balloon wagon." Further, the signal detachment received lessons on "repairing balloons, making netting" and handling small balloons with signal flags. Then the report somewhat casually remarked, "The balloon section, with gas generating and compressing machinery and storage tubes, was shipped to Fort Wadsworth, N.Y., on April 4, 1898."[132] That sentence of the report established that Fort Logan men and the balloon had entered the Spanish-American War with first duty on the East Coast. Thus Captain Glassford and Sergeant Ivy Baldwin had a surprising and sudden termination to their time at Fort Logan and, as it turned out, their time together.

In a prelude to the 1898 Spanish-American War, the United States had apprehensively watched unrest in Cuba for some years. In the late 1890s, the journalism of Hearst and Pulitzer fanned public interest in the island's political developments, with public sentiment largely supporting Cuban rebels fighting the Spanish government's rule. The military intervention by the United States was assured when the U.S. Navy's battleship *Maine* blew up in Havana's harbor on February 15, 1898. The sinking of the *Maine*, although of uncertain cause, sparked a demand for war against Spain, as it was believed that Spain was responsible. Congress passed a war resolution on April 19 and President McKinley signed it the next day. Spain declared war on the United States on April 24, and the United States responded with its formal proclamation of war against Spain on April 25. The proclamation had a retroactive date of April 21. The war began, and the invasion of Cuba with the Fort Logan balloon occurred in the following months.

The Spanish-American War blindsided Captain Glassford and Sergeant Ivy Baldwin and the whole Fort Logan balloon detachment. There had been little hint that a balloon might be involved in any hostilities with Spain. The work of Glassford and Baldwin, however, likely confirmed the balloon's readiness to be used as a reconnaissance vehicle in the war. Certainly, Sergeant Baldwin, virtually the lone army ascension specialist, would accompany the balloon to New York, but Captain Glassford would go to other Signal Corps duties. Thus Sergeant Ivy Baldwin was off to war, leaving his wife and the Denver balloon ascension season behind.

At the time of the initial deployment of Ivy Baldwin's balloon to New York, the Fort Logan balloon train had a balloon wagon, a supply wagon and three tube wagons for the 130 steel hydrogen tubes. In addition to the gas generator, the hydrogen tubes would provide for a reserve inflation.[133] The balloon detachment's assignment to Fort Wadsworth occurred because of the uncertain location of Spanish admiral Pascual Cervera's fleet, which had left the Cape Verde Islands headed west. This generated some fear that the fleet could attack the East Coast. The army believed the balloon could support coastal defense by detecting the approach of the hostile fleet to the New York Harbor area.

On the same day that the Fort Logan balloon was ordered to go to Fort Wadsworth, April 4, 1898, Sergeant Ivy Baldwin was quoted in a Denver newspaper, saying he laughed at Spanish guns. The subhead was "Intrepid Young Aeronaut Does Not Fear Either the Air or the Sea, and Is Anxious to Be Called to Fort Wadsworth for Active Duty."

When questioned by a reporter about a balloon being vulnerable to enemy fire near a frontline, Ivy stated, "The Spanish have no guns capable of striking a balloon at a height of 2,000 or 3,000 feet." He went on to acknowledge, however, that war against the Germans or French would be difficult: "They have made a special study of ballooning for war purposes and have guns which might prove very dangerous to an aeronaut studying their positions. An ordinary cannon is a dangerous thing to use for the purpose of bringing down a balloon....It requires a weapon made especially for the purpose. I have no fear of a rifle ball as the force of gravity acts directly upon a ball when it is fired."[134] Obviously, Ivy Baldwin was assuming observation of Spanish positions at a balloon height approximating 2,000 or 3,000 feet.

In the same article, Sergeant Baldwin said he would be in charge of the balloon he had built in Denver when it moved to Fort Wadsworth. He believed that at three thousand feet high, he would be able to see an enemy fleet approach New York Harbor at a distance of twenty-four miles. The paper said, "Sergeant Baldwin has made hundreds of ascensions in different parts of the world and made twelve ascensions on the sea shore near San Francisco, when he learned not to fear a drop into the briny ocean."[135]

At Fort Wadsworth, Major Joseph E. Maxfield became commander of the war balloon detachment. Simultaneously, the Signal Corps ordered the purchase of three more balloons with plans to have two balloon trains equipped with two war balloons each. Beyond these developments, little was accomplished at New York. Major Maxfield became busy with other Signal Corps duties, and Sergeant Baldwin said the unit "conducted a number of experiments in balloon signaling." When the Spanish fleet threat eased, Maxfield received orders to proceed with the balloon to Tampa, Florida, and the detachment departed New York on May 31, 1898.[136]

On arriving at Tampa, the war balloon and the support equipment were scattered in various railcars in the rail yard, but Maxfield had orders to go immediately to Santiago, Cuba. On the Tampa docks, he tried to assemble his personnel and equipment as best as he could. His command, now designated as the First Balloon Company, totaled three officers and twenty-four enlisted men, including Sergeant Ivy Baldwin.[137] To his dismay, Maxfield discovered that the unit had not been assigned a transport. Finally, on specific orders of Major General William R. Shafter, the Cuban expedition commander, they boarded the steamer *Rio Grande*. Once the balloon and equipment had been loaded (it took a day and a night), the twenty-seven-man detachment suffered a week's delay in leaving Tampa, sitting in tropical heat on the stifling ship. Ivy and Maxfield spread out the balloon, now newly named Santiago, on the deck. To their horror, they found that the heat had melted the balloon's varnish and that the sides had stuck together where folds existed. Even worse, the balloon silk looked to be rotting under the varnish. The *Rio*

Grande departed Tampa on June 14, 1898, and arrived at Cuba on June 22. The balloon company had to remain on ship more days, adding to the balloon's further deterioration.[138]

Major Maxfield, Sergeant Ivy Baldwin and the remainder of the Santiago's detachment finally went ashore at Daiquiri, Cuba, about eighteen miles east of Santiago, on June 28 without the balloon's gas-generating support. At that point, the company men knew they would have to use the reserve hydrogen tubes for filling the balloon, severely limiting further inflation possibilities.

General Shafter planned to deploy troops in the area of the Cuban port of Santiago as quickly as possible, but he knew nothing about the terrain or the disposition of enemy troops. Therefore, he saw the war balloon as a vital source of intelligence via aerial reconnaissance.

Sergeant Baldwin, with his balloon, wagons and gas tubes, began an advance toward Siboney, which was General Shafter's headquarters and a major expedition staging area. In an after-the-war interview, Ivy Baldwin said, "The roads were beastly, and it took us twenty-four hours to travel a distance of fifteen miles. It rained incessantly, and at night there was a dew as heavy as an ordinary rain. It was a hard pull to get the cylinders containing the gas over, as each one of them weighs from ninety to 100 pounds, and there's a good many of them."[139]

The next day, with some morning sunshine, Sergeant Baldwin and the men unpacked the balloon and again found that it had deteriorated further. Ivy said, "On spreading out the balloon it was found that the extreme hot weather had impaired its usefulness."[140] Major Maxfield would later claim, "In time of peace it would have been felt unsafe to use it."[141] Holes had to be sewed and covered with adhesive plaster to make the Santiago ready for ascension. Obviously, repair by the experienced Ivy Baldwin proved key to making any ascension possible. The balloon team began inflation using gas from the reserve hydrogen tubes.

Complying with General Shafter's orders, the balloon slowly moved to the front line. On June 30, three ascensions were made during the afternoon. Major Maxfield and Sergeant Baldwin made the first ascension at approximately four o'clock, primarily to assess the aerial worthiness of the Santiago. The second ascent had General Castillo of the Cuban rebels and Lieutenant W.S. Volkmar, one of Maxfield's officers, in the basket. The third flight included Maxfield and Shafter's chief engineer, Lieutenant Colonel George M. Derby. Derby wanted to scout roads and enemy positions before a planned attack at El Caney and San Juan Hill. The third ascension allowed Derby to collect information on "the streams and road between El Pozo and

San Juan Hill, and he and Maxfield confirmed the presence of the Spanish fleet in Santiago harbor."[142]

The next day, July 1, Lieutenant Colonel Derby told Maxfield that he wanted to make another ascension early in the morning. Ivy said he was "left below to look after the cable [tethering line]."[143] During the night, Baldwin had the Santiago sheltered in a low area and then, at daybreak, had his men use the last reserve gas to boost the balloon's lift. Additional holes and tears were patched. With this initial readiness, ropes were connected to the balloon and to a wagon, and the balloon moved about two miles down a road to El Pozo, where Maxfield and Derby boarded the basket. Although dangerously close to the firing line, Derby wanted the balloon to move forward to the front for better reconnaissance of Spanish positions near San Juan Hill. Maxfield protested that they were already too close to Spanish guns, but Derby pressed on. The road became so narrow and rough that Baldwin and crew abandoned the wagon and began walking the balloon forward, sometimes at only tree top level. The low altitude hampered Derby's observations, although some notes on terrain and Spanish emplacements were dropped to men below. After noticing the balloon, the Spanish troops began using the Santiago as an artillery marker and intensified their fire. Colonel Derby ordered the balloon higher, to about one thousand feet, but ropes and cable became entangled in brush, and as the ground crew frantically struggled, the Spanish fire, including that of rifles, intensified. Ivy Baldwin said, "Then they started to pepper us in good shape. They had discovered the balloon and commenced sending shrapnel into it. It was a warm place, but the boys never flinched."[144] The basket with Maxfield and Derby, at one point, was barely fifty feet in the air and a mere 650 yards from the Spanish riflemen. The Spanish shells and bullets began to find their mark, and the Santiago slowly descended and finally collapsed. Maxfield and Derby were able to jump out of the basket as it bounced to earth and escaped from the basket uninjured.

Noted author Stephen Crane, at the time a captain in the Tenth Cavalry at the front, wrote about the downing of the balloon: "The Balloon was dying, dying a gigantic and public death before the eyes of the two armies. It quivered, sank, faded into the trees amid the flurry of a battle that was suddenly and tremendously like a storm."[145]

After the descent and collapse of the Santiago shortly before eleven o'clock in the morning, Major Maxfield ordered Sergeant Baldwin and the ground crew to place the balloon and basket on the banks of a riverbed. Baldwin said Spanish fire became so hot that he and his men were ordered

When the Spanish-American War began in 1898, this Ivy Baldwin–constructed balloon was named Santiago. This photo captures one of its ascensions on the Cuban battle lines. *National Archives Photo.*

to retreat. "We dragged the balloon into the bed of the river and filled the basket with stones. This was done to keep it out of sight of the enemy." At this point, the detachment's only casualty occurred. "In retreating Private Haywood was shot through the foot, and we had to carry him back with us," said Baldwin. The Santiago detachment, in its withdrawal from the front, assisted in "carrying wounded and did related hospital work," according to Ivy.[146]

Later, Maxfield assigned a detachment lieutenant to go back to the riverbed and assess the damage to the balloon and determine what could be salvaged. The officer reported the numerous holes and tears in the air bag had made it useless for any further action. He folded the balloon, stuffed it back into its basket and on July 5 sent it to Siboney.[147] An after-the-war Signal Corps report stated, "The balloon was punctured in 13 places by small bullets," and there was evidence of shrapnel punctures.[148]

Major Maxfield went on to other Signal Corps duties, and the main body of the First Balloon Company departed captured Santiago harbor on

August 23. After arriving in New York, the detachment disbanded. However, equipment, hydrogen cylinders and the remains of Santiago remained at Montauk Point until September. Late in that month and into October 1898, the remnants of Santiago were exhibited at the Trans-Mississippi and International Exhibition in Omaha, Nebraska. Sergeant Ivy Baldwin went to the Omaha exhibition. The *Omaha Daily Bee* reported on October 4, 1898, that a portion of the Santiago balloon was "hanging from the ceiling" in the government exhibit hall. "At first it was thought it could be stretched out so as to show how badly it was riddled by Spanish bullets during the short time that it was in the air, but the coating of varnish on it has stuck together so tightly that it could not be spread out. As it hangs only a slight idea of its size can be obtained," said the newspaper.[149]

Members of the Second Balloon Company, which had never reached Cuba, were detailed to demonstrate ascensions at Omaha. With winter and the close of the exhibition in Nebraska, elements of the balloon corps went to Fort Myer, Virginia, as General Greely planned for that post to be the future home of the Signal Corps balloons.[150]

Sergeant Ivy Baldwin went on to Quincy, Illinois, on arriving back in the United States. During that time, he had interviews in which he was asked to comment on his Cuban balloon experience and the future of military balloons. "What do I think of the balloon in war? It is the coming ticket, and sure to be adopted by the government, the same as it has been by England, Germany and France," said Ivy. "The lessons learned at Santiago will prove of incalculable value in future experiments, and as it was I am sure it saved the lives of many who would have been sent out as scouts. We made complete plans of enemy's fortifications and had the lay of their entire surrounding army, which could never have been obtained in any other matter."[151]

The Santiago crew's success in reconnaissance proved much more limited than what Ivy Baldwin claimed. The observers had verified the location of Cervera's fleet and had discovered enemy positions and a new trail, thereby reducing military troop congestion on the main road to Santiago. This helped in the advance of two main troop elements.[152] However, the deployment of the balloon so close to the enemy fire lines and the low altitude observations greatly diminished the reconnaissance results and ultimately led to the war balloon's destruction. Furthermore, troops complained that the balloon drew killing bombardments on their positions, and members of the press asserted that the balloon gave the enemy a combat advantage. Theodore Roosevelt, leading the Rough Riders at the battle for San Juan Hill, later commented in his *Rough Rider* book that a captive balloon was up in the air at this moment but was worse than useless.

General Greely, despite these criticisms, believed the war experience had validated the Signal Corps' use of balloons, and he intended to keep a balloon corps. Unfortunately, in 1898, the Signal Corps balloon assets were placed in storage at Fort Myer, and the Signal Corps concentrated on other duties, such as communications and photography. In essence, the balloon corps continued to exist until the beginning of airplanes in the new century, but it was basically inactive.

After his time in Omaha and his leave in Illinois, Sergeant Ivy Baldwin reported to Fort Myer. He found the situation there far different from what he had experienced with Captain Glassford at Fort Logan in the late 1890s. In contrast to the ascensions and lively experimentation going on at Fort Logan, Ivy found a storage of balloons and equipment and an emphasis on signaling rather than on balloon operations. It seemed that war balloons had been shelved for a later day. It was no surprise, then, that at the beginning of 1901, when Ivy Baldwin's second enlistment was up, he separated from the army. Shortly thereafter, Ivy Baldwin returned to Denver.[153]

Sergeant Ivy Baldwin's experience in the Spanish-American War certainly ended on a low note. The balloon he and his wife personally fabricated had been destroyed. His great skills in balloon ascensions and repairs had been exploited only briefly. As he assessed the balloon's destruction and the military tactics employed in Cuba, he no doubt remembered Captain Glassford's admonitions about deploying a war balloon too close to the front lines, yet these had been ignored. Nevertheless, Ivy Baldwin continued to be enthusiastic about the future of military balloons and aerial reconnaissance in general. Even though his balloon skills seemed unneeded after the war, especially during the ensuing quiet times at Fort Myer, he never once lost his love of ascending into the heavens. He excitedly looked to resume his demonstration of aerial feats for the admiring Denver citizens.

5

BACK TO DENVER

Of course I realize the dangerous position I will be in with explosives and fireworks hanging from my trapeze.
—Denver Times, *1901*

The *Denver Post*, on June 10, 1901, carried a column with the headline "Hero of the Upper Air Coming Back to Denver: Sergeant Ivy Baldwin, Who Won Fame in the Spanish-American War as Aeronaut and High Diver, Will Build a Balloon Here." While the *Post* article mostly dealt with Ivy's war experience, it represented a public announcement that Ivy Baldwin was back in Denver.

Ivy quickly resumed his amusement park exhibitions. On July 14, 1901, the *Denver Times* reported on a balloon race between Baldwin and Frank Frazier, the black aeronaut, staged at Elitch's Gardens.[154] Ivy's association with Frazier began when he worked with Ivy as a sparker. Several men, called sparkers, usually stood by with buckets of water to douse any fire when a balloon began inflation from a fire pit. A balloon began to escape one day, and Frazier's foot got caught in a rope. Although scared out of his wits, he managed to get to a trapeze as the balloon soared, and he was able to ride the balloon down as it descended near the stockyards. Frazier seemed to take to the thrill of a balloon ascension and became a balloon performer.[155]

On July 24, 1901, the *Denver Post* began a story about "The Tall Man and the Short Man in a Balloon." The "tall man" was the *Post*'s Frank P. Sibley. He was accompanying Ivy Baldwin, the "short man," in a forthcoming balloon ascension.[156] The next day, the *Denver Post* announced that "The Post's Big Balloon Is Now Ready for the Ascension Next Sunday." The article had an accompanying photo of "Sergeant Ivy" positioned next to the balloon.[157] Three days later, the newspaper headlined that "Sergeant Ivy Baldwin and Frank P. Sibley of the Post Will Make the Greatest Ascent Ever Witnessed in Colorado from Elitch's Gardens This Afternoon about Four O'Clock…Scientific Observations to Be Made." The article sought to add excitement by posing questions: "Where will they land?" and "What awful experiences await them?" Mr. Sibley expected to use a heliograph to send flashes of Morse code and to employ other scientific instruments, a camera and notebooks. Ivy, on the other hand, anticipated sitting on the anchor two hundred feet below the basket, "where he can enjoy a quiet smoke without danger of igniting the balloon overhead."[158]

The *Post*'s scientific balloon enterprise was more memorable than expected. Reminiscent of the Buckwalter balloon episode in 1894, the balloon got aloft without Baldwin on board. The next day's papers carried a "Vivid Description of a Wild Ride" by Mr. Sibley. It reported that the ascension occurred as a storm developed with flashing lightning and rain. Needless to say, no scientific exercises occurred. With frightening speed and a "Hazardous Descent to Earth," the terrified Sibley, alone in the basket, "came down on the ranch of John Hall, halfway between Castle Rock and Parker in Douglas County." The newspaper proclaimed that Sibley's thirty-one-mile trip in an hour and forty minutes constituted a "Record for the Longest Balloon Journey Out of Denver."[159]

In mid-August, Elitch's planned a celebration of Ivy Baldwin's 2,000th aerial ascension. The *Denver Times* commented, "Mrs. Elitch Long [Elitch's Gardens owner], with characteristic enterprise, intends making the occasion a notable one."[160] The amusement park planned a great display of fireworks with Ivy Baldwin firing rockets, and his ascension was to be illuminated by a powerful searchlight. The day before the affair, Baldwin reportedly said, "Of course I realize the dangerous position I will be in with explosives and fireworks hanging from my trapeze."[161]

The exhibition of fireworks proved spectacular for the seven thousand in attendance, with a huge tower "gorgeously illuminated with colored lights" and huge fire posts on top that "discharged a shower of stars in every direction." According to the *Denver Times*, "Sergeant Baldwin started on his flight with a frame filled with red, white, and blue fire," and when the balloon reached 1,500 feet, he set off a "fresh supply of fireworks." At that point, a strong wind caught the balloon, blowing it to the northwest, and

A Baldwin balloon liftoff occurs at Denver's Elitch's Gardens as a summer highlight. Balloon ascensions at amusement parks attracted crowds for many years in the late nineteenth and early twentieth centuries. *History Colorado Collection.*

a "cold blast struck the hot air bag and it collapsed." As the balloon fell, it was shredded as it dragged across a barbed wire fence, and resilient Baldwin escaped with only severe scratches.[162]

Undeterred by this mishap on his 2,000th ascension, Ivy planned for a balloon launch on August 19 that would set a new altitude record. A strong wind terminated that attempt, however.[163]

The busy aeronaut then turned to tower jumping on August 23 and 25, with the added razzle-dazzle of fireworks attached to his body. Baldwin had planned to wear an asbestos suit to protect him from the powder and flames, but he was unable to find such clothing in the city. In keeping with his trend of carrying out announced performances, he elected to sew fireworks onto his clothes. He climbed the 125-foot tower, and as he stood at the top, an assistant torched the fireworks. "With the flames burning his skin and skyrockets whizzing throughout the air and before his eyes he stepped out on

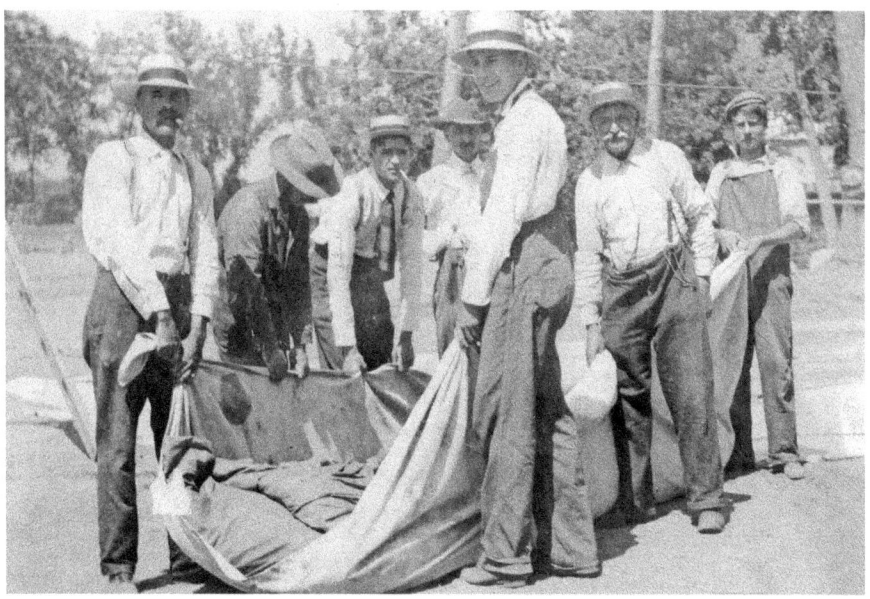

Men help move a deflated balloon. Ivy Baldwin successfully recruited ordinary citizens and spectators to help him move his equipment. *History Colorado Collection.*

the little platform, stood on his hands and dived head first for the net below. Like a comet he went through the air, the fireworks blazing and sputtering all about him, struck the net, an assistant quenched the flames and he strolled to his dressing room as if nothing had happened." The next day, the public "learned that he had been confined to his bed" because of his burns.[164]

Another notable event occurred in October 1901, when Baldwin provided his balloon expertise to support photojournalist Harry Buckwalter's contract to do an aerial photograph of the famous Georgetown, Colorado rail loop. The Colorado and Southern Railroad engaged Buckwalter, at considerable expense, to do aerial shots of the complete loop, while Baldwin contributed the balloon and the inflation equipment, costing over $400. The balloon and the chemicals and gear to do the inflation were positioned at a small rocky bench near the middle of the loop, overlooking the town to the north. The inflation began at daybreak on October 27, when Ivy Baldwin and four small boys started the gas tank in preparation for connection to the balloon. Continuous high winds at the site made Ivy and many others nervous. "Seven hundred people from Georgetown and the adjacent country watched the battle between Buckwalter and the wind.…Women in many hued raiment and men in Sunday clothes formed brilliant color effects against the cold gray mountains," claimed a newspaper.

Near noon, Buckwalter and his camera stepped into the basket. A shout of "heave off" was heard, and the men desperately holding the ropes loosened their grip a bit, but the balloon did not rise. In some belated reflection, Baldwin and Buckwalter believed the 210-pound photographer might be part of the problem. Baldwin pumped more gas into the balloon, and after another half hour, he prepared to get into the basket. At that moment, the notorious Georgetown wind roared down on the site. A reporter said, "It swooped down upon the huge balloon and whirled it around like a top. It raised it up and dashed it back again." A gust hit the bag squarely and tore a hole four feet long.[165]

As a testament to Buckwalter's camera skills, he managed to obtain some remarkable photographs of the balloon's inflation and initial rise. All agreed that because of the treacherous winds, any photographing of the Georgetown Loop would need to take place in the summer. This second collaboration of Ivy Baldwin and Harry Buckwalter, much like the first in 1894, had developed into a frightening episode with a very lucky ending.[166]

"The only 'honeymoon flight' from Elitch's Gardens ended quite unromantically in a severe wind and rain storm atop Table Mountain near Golden where Baldwin brought the balloon down. He and the drenched couple were brought back to Denver by horse-drawn wagon," reported a local community newspaper.[167]

Ivy Baldwin continued various and similar exhibitions at Denver's amusement parks during the succeeding summer seasons. The effort to keep the thrill factor in events intensified the hazards he faced. The danger in balloon operations was especially highlighted in May 1902, when balloonist Ben Bowen died in an ascension at Manhattan Beach amusement park. The *Denver Post* headlined "Ben Bowen, Despite Advice and Pleadings, Ascends in His Balloon at Manhattan Beach—Struck by the Wind, He Drops into the Water and Is Drowned."[168] A later news publication reported that Ivy Baldwin had been angered by a newspaper writer, who said balloon ascensions ought to be stopped because Ben Bowen had lost his life at Manhattan Beach the other day.

In August 1902, Ivy decided to add a new wrinkle to his balloon performances. He would take his tethered balloon, called Old Glory, as high as 1,500 feet and then slide down a cable to the ground. His first attempt at this trick, before a huge Sunday crowd at Elitch's, produced some injuries that could have been much worse. A newspaper described what happened:

AVIATOR, AERIALIST & AERONAUT

Last Sunday when Ivy Baldwin made the ascent, preparatory to his slide, the air was calm and everything seemed most auspicious. But after he had begun the descent a gust of wind suddenly took a hand in the performance and changed the program materially. The canvas bag began to sway to and fro and Mr. Baldwin's trip became more hazardous, the rubber grip which protects his hands became warmer and warmer until a stop was necessary, some 800 feet in the air, to allow the grip to cool. As soon as this was affected he made another start, but at a perilous moment, for then the balloon made a dash and the cable passed between his legs. Nearly all the exposed points had been padded by Mr. Baldwin, preparatory to his dangerous undertaking, but the cable managed to find an unprotected spot. The burn extended for six inches on the inside of his left leg and proved a most painful injury.[169]

A balloon inflation begins at Colorado's famous Georgetown Loop railroad site in October 1901. Photographer Harry H. Buckwalter was to take aerial photographs of the Loop from a Baldwin-provided balloon under contract with the railroad. *Harry H. Buckwalter Collection, History Colorado.*

Spectators stand on the Georgetown Loop high bridge watching efforts to get the Baldwin balloon aloft for the Buckwalter aerial photographs of the railroad site. *Harry H. Buckwalter Collection, History Colorado.*

Aviator, Aerialist & Aeronaut

Above: Ivy Baldwin provided the balloon and equipment for the Buckwalter aerial photographic contract at the Georgetown Loop, and inflation initially seemed to be a success. *Harry H. Buckwalter Collection, History Colorado.*

Right: High winds hit the Georgetown Loop balloon ascension and propelled the gas bag against rocks, destroying it and causing the failure to complete the Buckwalter contract. *Harry H. Buckwalter Collection, History Colorado.*

Typically, Baldwin claimed his injuries were "all in the business," and he was already making arrangements for another slide performance. He remarked, however, that he would review his padding distribution. He went on to say, "The general impression has been that I hold the cable with my feet as well as my hands, but this would be too impractical." He was indicating that his slide feat contained far more hand strength and slide savvy than the average onlooker thought. Despite the necessary stops to cool the hands and relax tense muscles, Baldwin asserted, "It is a heap more fun than making an ascent over Santiago with 10,000 Spanish soldiers taking pot shots at you."[170]

Also in 1902, considerable publicity developed around an attempt to fly a balloon from Denver to New York, piloted by Tom Baldwin and Percy Hudson. It was hoped that the balloon flight would break many world records. For the event, the *Denver Post* sponsored a huge balloon named Big Glory, which had a height of 105 feet. It was launched at Elitch's Gardens on September 1, with an alleged half million spectators watching. Fierce winds quickly pushed Big Glory southward toward Pike's Peak. Currents lifted it to 28,000 feet and sent it through canyons and forests. The next day, the newspaper reported, "After a long and hopeless battle against the tremendous odds of raging storms and contrary winds, the Post's balloon, Big Glory, was finally compelled to land in a bleak mountain wilderness about twenty-six miles northwest of Florence, Colo." The balloon voyageurs were said to have been "half frozen, half dead from exhaustion."[171] Although Ivy Baldwin did not participate in this ill-fated flight, he no doubt took notice and carefully weighed what went wrong.

During this first decade of the 1900s, Ivy Baldwin's family expanded with the birth of another son, Harry E. Baldwin, in 1902 and the birth of a daughter, Helen (called Ila) Baldwin, in 1905.[172] More family members meant Ivy had to continue with his amusement park adventures, as these venues constituted his livelihood. On August 25, 1907, he recorded his 2,512th ascent at Elitch's Gardens.

Baldwin and the amusement parks always remained conscious of the need to provide fresh, new and thrilling events to keep paying customers coming month after month and season after season. One technique was to emphasize attaining a new record of some kind. For example, on July 4, 1909, Ivy announced that he planned a balloon ascension with the "Hope to Reach Altitude of Twenty-Five Thousand Feet."[173] Another lure was to incorporate a performance with an unusual twist or some scientific endeavor. Just such an event occurred on July 19, 1909, when Baldwin collaborated with the Colorado National Guard Signal Corps to demonstrate various

Ivy Baldwin in his Elitch's Gardens workshop in 1907. *History Colorado Collection.*

signaling devices between the balloon aloft and the ground crews. A curious feature of this exercise was making an "Observation Under Water." Balloon occupants flew over a nearby lake and took notes on sighting objects deep in the water. Supposedly, this could show the value of a tethered balloon at U.S. ports in wartime to spot a hostile submarine.[174]

Still, it was Ivy Baldwin's stunts, or at times misadventures, that attracted the public's attention. His reputation continued to grow. On August 16, 1909, he was referred to as "being the nerviest man in the world" when he made a balloon trip holding on to the trailing rope. A city newspaper said, "It was the most hazardous ascension ever made at Elitch's Gardens."[175]

While risky balloon ascensions and tower jumps remained staples of Baldwin's amusement park performances for many years, a number of events foreshadowed changes to come. In 1903, the Wright brothers' flight of a powered, heavier-than-air aircraft captured the interest and imagination of the nation. At last, an answer to controlled flight seemed to be at hand. Also, in 1904, Ivy watched the new dirigible developments by his former partner and mentor Thomas S. Baldwin. In addition, the amusement park environment had become ever more competitive. Even a protégé of Baldwin, Wayne Abbott, began many exhibitions.

So, energetic and enterprising Ivy Baldwin began to look at the potential of dirigible or airplane flights in his future performances.

6
AIRSHIPS AND AIRPLANES

The nose shot upward. The bag tossed again, then suddenly shot away....
Suddenly a sheet of flame shot across the sky. In another instant came a deafening
report, and then a great ball of fire. The big ship had exploded.
—Kansas City Journal, *1906*

Ivy Baldwin closely observed the aerial activities of his former partner Thomas Scott Baldwin in the early 1900s. Tom Baldwin had ignited an airship craze in the United States with his dirigible experiments from 1904 to 1909. During that period, his airships made 193 ascents, with 174 successful round trips. Also, he had sold a powered airship to the army in 1908. Tom Baldwin tried a pedal-powered elongated balloon as early as 1892, though it failed, as did a follow-on dirigible powered with a twenty-four-horsepower automobile engine. The latter had notable air control problems. Tom's California Arrow, however, constructed in San Jose, California, became the first real navigable airship in the United States. The fifty-two-foot-long and seventeen-foot-diameter cigar-shaped dirigible, powered by a seven-horsepower Curtiss motorcycle engine and an eight-foot propeller, successfully flew a closed course over San Francisco Bay from Oakland's Idora Park on August 4, 1904. After the initial flight, Baldwin decided to hand off the piloting to A. Roy Knabenshue. There had been other American airships in this time period, but the California Arrow proved to be the best known, and it pioneered the way for further airship development.[176]

Ivy Baldwin began constructing an almost exact replica of the California Arrow in 1905. The cutting and sewing of approximately five hundred yards of silk, followed by multiple coats of varnish, took about six months and cost nearly $2,500. After the fat cigar-shaped bag took shape, Ivy added over-the-top netting with ropes extending below to suspend a long, narrow platform for the pilot, motor and steering mechanism. This platform hung below the air bag at a distance that hopefully prevented igniting the gas from the hot engine. The expected lifting power was four hundred pounds. When approaching readiness for flight test, the non-rigid dirigible's length reached fifty-two feet, with a diameter of seventeen feet. It had a capacity of eight thousand cubic feet of hydrogen or illuminating gas. A six-horsepower gasoline engine linked to a ten-foot-by-fourteen-inch propeller powered the craft. At best, meaning in still air, it could allegedly reach a speed of twelve miles per hour.[177]

The Ivy Baldwin dirigible had its own building "expressly built for it" outside of the grounds and adjoining the "circus lot" of Elitch's Gardens. Baldwin thoughtfully named the airship Elitch in honor of the Elitch's Gardens owner. This seemed more than appropriate, as a newspaper article reported that in "casting around the country for a decided novelty Mrs. Elitch Long decided on an airship and a study of the various ships soon convinced her that Baldwin's was the only one which would be successful in every particular." Furthermore, continued the newspaper, "With the improvements that are being made upon it the huge air craft should be more perfect when it makes its first flight at Elitch's than any other airship in the world." Optimistically, the paper maintained, "The Baldwin ship has solved the problem of aerial navigation."[178]

Two weeks before the planned Elitch's 1906 summer exhibition, Ivy Baldwin made a flight test that was termed a "remarkably successful flight." According to the *Denver Post*, "From the moment he left the ground Baldwin had perfect control of the vessel. He circled around, first to the right and then to the left, going higher or lower as he willed. The weather was ideal, with only a slight wind blowing. This he sailed against with as much ease as he sailed with it."[179]

The ending of his first test flight, though successful, turned out to be less than perfect. After a half hour in the air, Ivy "pointed the nose toward the ground and made a splendid descent." He noticed, however, that the Elitch was coming down near where a crowd had gathered, and "realizing the probability of hurting someone, he changed his course and brought the ship safely to the ground about one block from outside of the fence." Men walked the Elitch to its barn.

Colorado's Daring Ivy Baldwin

A report said, "Prof. Baldwin is well pleased with his demonstrations and declares that under anything like favorable conditions he can repeat the performance." At about this same time, as many as nine other Colorado individuals planned to construct and fly airships, but Ivy Baldwin ended up building and flying the first powered airship in the state.[180] Also notable in this first successful demonstration was how deftly Baldwin piloted his airship. If he had received instructions in piloting a dirigible, he never recorded it. This new skill seemed to mirror his other flying experiences in that he was apparently able to master flying largely by instinct.

Ivy Baldwin pictured in his more mature years but still a performing aeronaut. *Carnegie Library for Local History, Boulder, Colorado.*

The Baldwin airship had periodic engine problems, but the main trouble was with the wind. Another flight of Elitch in June 1906, which lured a huge crowd, nearly ended in tragedy. After Ivy had started a flight, a stiff breeze began, and he wisely decided to return the airship to its hangar. As the craft struggled in the wind and started to descend, anxious witnesses sought to grab ropes to help bring it under control just as it came over a ridge at the back of the amusement park. A gust hit the envelope broadside, twisting it and breaking ropes. Baldwin frantically tried to release the Elitch's gas, but as the air bag deflated, an explosion occurred, collapsing and seriously damaging the airship. Fortunately, despite the fall, Ivy and others on the ground escaped injury.[181]

Undaunted by this event, he rebuilt the Elitch, and in October, he took it to Kansas City, Missouri, for a series of scheduled exhibitions at the city's fairgrounds. During the second ascension, on October 6, 1906, Ivy encountered troubling winds. He weighed the wisdom of another flight as he "stood beside his big airship, as it swayed and billowed in the wind....A dozen men were clinging to the frail frame." But Baldwin reasoned that everything had been tested, including the engine, and the proper ballast was aboard. Also, he never wanted to cancel a scheduled performance.

As he mounted the triangular platform, the "big yellow torpedo tossed and rolled." Ivy shouted, "Let her go." Then "the engine puffed. The ship started but was swung around by the wind. The dozen helpers hung tight and pulled the big balloon back to the starting place."

"I can't make it," Ivy said. "But let's take another try."

Baldwin repeated his command "to let go."

The men released the ropes. "The nose shot upward. The bag tossed again, then suddenly shot away....Suddenly a sheet of flame shot across the sky. In another instant came a deafening report, and then a great ball of fire. The big ship had exploded." The propeller had cut a hole in the air bag, and the engine exhaust ignited the escaping gas.

A reporter at the site gave the following account: "Its nose was probably thirty feet from the ground. Out of the mass of smoke and flame shot the form of a man—Baldwin. Round about him tumbled the burning pongee silk, 500 yards of it, oil soaked. On his hands and knees he crawled from the firey debris, kicking himself loose from the tangling net. He staggered to his feet, tumbled over, got up again, and then fell into the arms of two policemen."

Ivy and his mechanic, Jim Mathews, who was the last man to let go of a rope, were taken to a tent behind the grandstand to check their injuries. Ivy sustained a burned right hand; a scorched neck; singed mustache, hair and eyebrows; and a bruised body. His mechanic had bruised legs.

A severely depressed Ivy Baldwin, looking at the burning wreckage, was heard remarking, "There it is." Someone asked how much the loss was, and Baldwin replied, "About $2,500…there are 500 yards of silk, an engine worth $1,000, and about six months of mighty hard work." Another bystander asked about insurance, to which Ivy replied, "No…they don't insure things that are not down on the ground or the water."[182]

The flaming, disastrous end of Elitch thoroughly shook Ivy Baldwin. He had survived a thirty-foot fall, an explosion and seemingly certain death. His six-month investment of time and his meager savings had gone up in smoke and debris. He decided he would not build another airship, and he seriously considered giving up flying altogether.[183]

Perhaps entering into Ivy's heightened sense of mortality was an incident that occurred only some months before. Several newspapers, including the *Houston Daily Post*, had reported his death in an explosion of a balloon in Ohio. The September 1905 paper headlined, "Ivy Baldwin, Aeronaut, Met His Death While Suspended in the Clouds." A subhead added, "Dynamite Exploded and Remains of Man and Machine Were Scattered Over a Wide Area."

Later, when confronted with the story, Ivy explained that the dead balloonist had been making ascensions as "one of the original Baldwins," and assumptions had been made that it was Ivy. Adding to the possibility that the victim was Ivy Baldwin was the news that the balloonist had dynamite on board in an effort to make the ascension like the war experience during the charge up San Juan Hill.[184]

Two months after the false reports of Ivy's death, an interview of Ivy Baldwin, while he was in Houston visiting his mother, reported that he was "Working on Aeroplane Through Which He Expects to Solve Air Navigation Problem."[185] This indicated early on that Ivy, noting the Wright flying experiments, saw the great possibilities of airplanes.

Although Ivy's troubles with his airships had convinced him that he needed to return to his trusted balloon ascensions, the airship had eclipsed the balloon's popularity in amusement park exhibitions during the first decade of the 1900s. This period of powered dirigible balloons proved rather short, though. On the horizon, the development of the airplane, beginning with the Wright brothers' aircraft in 1903, seemed to offer a better answer to the age-old problem of controlled flight. Nevertheless, the balloon-type airships had provided a significant bridge between balloon ascensions and the airplane. Not only did the airships strengthen piloting skills and aeronautical knowledge, but they also kept the names of pilots, such as Tom and Ivy Baldwin, in the newspapers. Flight by any means continued to fascinate a large segment of the population.[186]

It is difficult to determine the extent of Ivy Baldwin's knowledge of the Wright airplane experiments. Certainly, by various statements, he followed the development of the powered, fixed-wing aircraft. With his great understanding of the forces involved in flying, he could easily grasp the possibilities of the Wright plane. He would not hesitate to tackle this new aerial machine.

By 1909, several developments converged to bring a major shift in Ivy's home state of Colorado. During previous years, a number of men in the state had failed in attempts to build a workable aircraft. By following the lead of the Wright brothers, airplane builders began to combine "propulsion, airfoils, and control mechanisms in a successful product." At the same time, profit prospects increased, attracting more financial support.[187] This prompted new organizations to actively promote aerial contests with an emphasis on setting new records. The *Denver Post*, in 1909, announced a $10,000 prize for "successful flying machine demonstrations." On July 30, the paper headlined, "All Kinds of Airships Entered in Contest—State Will Receive Remarkable Amount of Advertising Through Tests to Be Made Here."[188]

In response to the $10,000 incentive, several Colorado residents announced plans to compete for the prize, including George C. Ady, a Denver electrical engineer, who hoped to enter an aircraft with Ivy Baldwin's help. The *Post* reported those two men "are at work at Elitch's Gardens on a by-plane, a flying machine they think will eclipse all others."[189]

Ironically, the next day, the newspaper said that Ady and Baldwin "are determined that they are going to carry off the Post's $10,000 prize for successful flying machine demonstration," but they were beginning this effort with a balloon ascension. "Sunday, they are to make an ascension in the Post balloon at Elitch's Gardens for the purpose of studying the currents, that they may be aided in building their creature of the air. They hope to ascend 25,000 feet into the ether." According to the report, pure hydrogen would be used to reach such a height.[190] This turn to balloons seemed to be related to a notice that members of the Aero Club in Denver planned to make a "series of balloon ascensions to make aerial observation which will acquaint them with the exact air current conditions in this latitude."[191]

This Ady-Baldwin balloon ascension to study air currents as a precursor to building an aircraft only succeeded in reaching twenty thousand feet. However, this proved very important to Ivy, as he claimed he had discovered an air current flowing easterly. Apparently, this news excited "the Post's flying machine editor," and he and "Major Ivy Baldwin" were to make another high-altitude balloon ascension the following week. It was the belief of the two balloonists that Ivy might again discover and fly this river of air leading to all manner of records. The newspaper said, "The Post balloon may come down on the Atlantic coast, which will be breaking of every substantiated balloon record both for duration and distance flights."[192]

Ivy Baldwin's elaborate plan for studying the strata of air currents via a high-altitude balloon provided insights into his intelligence and aeronautical thinking. He proposed to build an "auxiliary bag" in the main balloon envelope. The newspaper described the arrangement:

> In order to insure [sic] *a record-breaking trip,* Major Baldwin has equipped his Post balloon with an auxiliary bag.... The auxiliary bag is a balloon itself, about one-third as large as the main balloon, and is to be attached to the middle of the larger bag in such a way that the gas lost from the big bag by expansion in the warmer air currents will be turned directly into the smaller balloon and thus prevent the loss of any lifting power. When

the cooler currents of air are reached and cause contraction of the gas, ordinarily causing the balloon to drop, the surplus gas will be turned back into the main balloon and the lifting power maintained.

The effect of this new arrangement will be the absence of the gas fluctuation, which is fatal to long trips in the air of gas balloons. Theoretically the arrangement should enable the balloon to remain in the air indefinitely.[193]

Baldwin also intended to boost the balloon's lift by using pure hydrogen. A hydrogen plant was built at Elitch's for this purpose. Reportedly, forty-five thousand cubic feet of hydrogen had been made to "give lifting power five times as great as illuminating coal gas."[194]

By such extensive preparations for exploring air currents, Ivy Baldwin demonstrated his powerful knowledge of lifting power and the impact of the ever-changing air streams. He saw benefits in airplane building by obtaining a better understanding of these forces. In a remarkable discussion at the time, he elaborated on his views about aircraft construction and airplane flight at Denver's high altitude. "It is difficult to construct a flying machine that is to be tested in the west," he said. "It is necessary to make the machine much larger or else much lighter than one intended for use at sea level. Our aerial machine is to be a two-passenger one, with two propellers, operated by a fifty-horsepower engine. Select spruce from Oregon will be the lightest and yet the strongest to be obtained. Forty by thirty-five feet will be its dimensions."[195] Obviously, Ady and Baldwin had a bigger and more powerful aircraft than a Wright model in mind.

Also, Baldwin had considered the cost of building such an ambitious entry for the *Post* contest. "The new material alone for such an aeroplane costs $3,000, and before the completion I am sure it will run up $2,000," said Ivy. This relatively large sum was destined to impact later aircraft developments.

Meanwhile, it was back to the immediate balloon ascension. "The building of the ship important as it is, is not so important as thorough knowledge of the vagaries of the currents in this atmosphere," declared Baldwin in a news article. Despite this preliminary concentrated interest on air currents and lift, the fabrication of a plane was expected to proceed, and there was an optimistic construction time as well. "Within two months we will construct it at Elitch's Gardens, where every convenience has been offered us by Mrs. Elitch-Long," Ivy announced.[196]

The highly publicized balloon ascension to study air currents using Baldwin's new balloon design failed. At the same time, the Ady-Baldwin aircraft experienced major problems, and the high cost plagued the project.

No airworthy machine materialized in 1909. The next year, aeronauts and aviators from outside Colorado came for demonstrations and for the possibility of winning contests. On February 1, 1910, Louis Paulhan, born in France, came to Denver from air shows in Los Angeles and Salt Lake City and made a flying exhibition with a Farman III aircraft at Overland Park, Denver's racetrack. He became the first individual to fly an airplane in Colorado. On two succeeding days, he flew before enthusiastic crowds but crashed into a fence on the third day, injuring several bystanders but escaping injury himself.[197] Later that summer, other out-of-state pilots with various aircraft did exhibition flights. On July 22, 1910, W.L. Marr and E. Linn Mathewson flew their own locally built Curtiss-type biplane from a site on Monaco Boulevard in the Park Hill neighborhood. In its best effort, it only flew for one hundred yards at a height of twenty feet, but it represented the first flight of a Colorado-built plane.[198]

In November, noted Wright aviator team of Walter Brookins, Ralph Johnston and Arch Hoxsey arrived in Denver and conducted exhibitions at Overland Park. These flyers had established some aerial records and succeeded in dominating the local aviation scene. With this influx of outsiders, Ivy Baldwin lost any pioneering role in flying airplanes in his home state. Moreover, now his exploits were overshadowed by other pilots and would-be airplane builders.

No firm date has been established at to when Ivy Baldwin learned to pilot an airplane. When asked when he had his first airplane ride, he replied, "Well, that I made myself, in my own plane." The place he stated was in San Francisco:

> *There was three of us got together, and we built a plane that was a copy of the Curtiss. And it was up to me to fly it. They were carpenters and I wasn't, and they turned the plane over to me to fly it. I made a number of small flights in it, you know, say up to 100 feet or something of that kind, and maybe fly for two or three minutes. Some days we couldn't fly a tall. If the day was hot, the sun was shining good and hot, it was hard to get off the ground. But if it was a cloudy day, or a rainy day, it was easy to fly. You could fly much easier then.*[199]

Baldwin understood that air proved heavier in cooler conditions and thus aided flight.

He also told a story in which he mentioned a timeline of about "three years ago," indicating 1910, when he attempted to "fly over the Golden Gate out in 'Frisco.'"

"Some flight," Ivy stated, "that I started as enthusiastic as a newlywed, but before I had gone over half a mile and was just preparing to rise on my high horse, ready to leap the gate, something happened. I don't remember just what did happen and it seems that a telegraph pole had run into me in some way or other because I had wrapped the aeroplane about the said pole....I didn't fly the Golden Gate. I did spend several weeks by request in the hospital nursing a few broken bones."[200] It seems likely that Baldwin, as in the case of the airship, had never received airplane piloting instruction. He just learned by doing it.

He must have conquered the Curtiss pusher to a degree that he felt comfortable entering a Nevada flying demonstration. In June 1910, Baldwin and companions shipped their aircraft (some called it a Curtiss-Paulhan airplane) by rail to Carson City, Nevada, to enter the Carson City Sagebrush Carnival program. He and his crew reassembled their plane at nearby Raycraft Ranch, while advertisements circulated about daily flights planned by Ivy Baldwin. On June 23, 1910, Ivy made the first airplane flight in the state of Nevada, which eventually earned him a place of honor in the Nevada Aerospace Hall of Fame.[201]

One can discern a more mature Ivy Baldwin in this photograph. His gentlemanly demeanor belied a fierce determination to perform at the highest level. *History Colorado Collection.*

Baldwin and others harbored doubts about a successful flight at Carson City's 4,675-foot altitude, which was far different from flights at sea level near San Francisco. Nevertheless, he attained a max height of about 50 feet as he flew for approximately a half mile before he turned back with a successful landing. At a total of 4,725 feet mean sea level, the flight momentarily claimed a new altitude record. Ivy followed with carnival exhibition flights on July 3, 4 and 5.[202]

Ivy's aviation activities became unusually quiet for a period after the Nevada success. The reason or reasons are not clear. He returned to Denver, and he may have had airplane problems. He was likely working with a number of amateur builders beset with many technical and financial headaches.

For example, in 1910, the General Aviation Company began in Denver. It quickly made known that it intended to build and sell aircraft, but the lack of a market soon forced it into sponsoring exhibition flying. In 1913, the company built a copy of a Wright biplane and equipped it with pontoons. Reports said, "The machine has been tested several times, with unsatisfactory results, mainly because of the inexperience of the aviator employed by the company." The owners, including Arthur C. Wager, the company vice president, who constructed the plane, then recruited Ivy Baldwin to pilot the airplane from the Manhattan Beach amusement park. Manhattan Beach had emerged as the leading competitor of Elitch's Gardens, beginning in 1891. Baldwin flew the hydroplane for the first time on May 18. "It sailed across the lake [Sloan's Lake] without hitch and rose in the air like a huge bird." Ivy circled the lake once at a height of fifteen feet and started to make another circle at approximately forty feet. Just as the General Aviation Company owners were congratulating themselves on the shoreline for Baldwin's success, a sound indicated that something snapped, and suddenly, the plane plunged into the water. As the machine hit, one pontoon broke, tilting the craft to one side, half submerging the plane, and Baldwin was thrown into the lake. He grabbed a guywire to keep his head above water and shouted for help. A rowboat came from the shore to rescue him. Later, helpers towed the plane to shore.[203]

Later in the summer, Baldwin got the hydroaeroplane airborne off the lake on weekends and holidays, but he had other crashes into Sloan's Lake. On June 13, he took off in the General Aviation plane, despite warnings from friends that it was Friday the thirteenth. "The hydro-aeroplane, after sweeping gracefully about the rim of the lake at an altitude of 75 feet suddenly sprung a wing." Ivy desperately tried to control the machine, "but the air craft darted like an arrow, nose downward, for the water." Ivy managed to get to a bog-like area on the lake's rim. Pontoons and other plane elements were scattered nearby. Rescuers remarked that Ivy seemed far more concerned that the engine had gotten wet than about any injuries he might have sustained.[204]

As the summer of 1913 came to an end, Ivy made an unusual decision to abandon flying airplanes. One could assume that the several crashes in the hydroaeroplane led to this major change. That was not the case, however. In a much later interview, Baldwin indicated that his termination decision came as a result of an argument with the manager of the General Aviation Company. He said, "After I perfected the plane [a copy of the Wright plane] and wanted to take it out and work fairs and carnivals with it, why, the manager of what he called, let's see, what was the...General Aviation Company, well, he was the manager. And he wouldn't let me take the plane away from Manhattan Beach, and as him and I got into quite an argument and I quit the company altogether. I haven't touched a plane since. I got disgusted with him. I went back to tight rope walking and ballooning."[205]

It remains difficult to imagine Ivy Baldwin giving up on any flying experience. He eagerly seized opportunities to get into the air, whether it was via balloons, balloon-type dirigibles or airplanes. It seems likely that other factors entered into his airplane flying decision beside his personal argument with the General Aviation Company manager. As previously noted, pilots of various aircraft began to crowd the amusement park exhibitions, diminishing Ivy's popularity and business opportunities. In contrast to his ability to construct his own balloons, the cost and complexity of aircraft construction meant that he was at the mercy of others for capital and engineering expertise. Moreover, any airplane crash could lead to a financial disaster. In sum, Ivy Baldwin did not have the resources to almost singlehandedly command the air show as he once did. Coinciding with these airplane-related developments, the possibility of employment developed at the Eldorado Springs resort—a relatively short distance from Boulder, Colorado. He could return to his early days of tightrope walking and ballooning, leaving behind his obvious frustrations associated with his airplane experiences.

Although Ivy Baldwin had largely lost his pioneering role in flying airplanes to other pilots, he established three notable records. He flew the first aircraft in the state of Nevada, piloted the first airship in Colorado and flew the first hydroplane or seaplane in Colorado. In these accomplishments he managed to survive horrible explosions, falls and crashes. However, in typical fashion, he would courageously recover from such deadly mishaps with the determination to try again. Finally, the airplane seemed to present obstacles in his usual repeat performances. Nevertheless, he never wavered in his belief that the airplane represented the future and that man's flight across the sky was an exhilarating adventure. Now, perhaps age, at last, led him to let others do the flying.

7

ELDORADO SPRINGS

I didn't think he would make it when he climbed up to the wire, but, once he was on the wire and started across, he was his usual spectacular self.
—Rocky Mountain News, *Denver, 1953*

Even as Ivy Baldwin flew airplanes, he returned to performances on the tightrope. These represented a throwback to his first daring feats on the wire in the San Antonio, Texas area as a young boy. On June 7, 1907, at the age of forty-one, he made the first of eighty-six spectacular crossings at the entrance to South Boulder Canyon at Eldorado Springs.[206] This began a long relationship with this resort location approximately twenty-five miles northwest of Denver and on the southwest edge of the city of Boulder.

Denver businessman Frank Fowler and four partners formed the Moffat Lakes Resort Company, acquired the Eldorado Springs site in South Boulder Canyon and, by 1905, began developing the recreation area into a summer resort.[207] Fowler and his associates intended to attract visitors to the hot springs on the floor of the relatively narrow canyon, which also had a fast-flowing stream. This resort business was new to the Moffat Lakes Company partners, but they believed that with Frank Fowler's vision and his skills, they would succeed. In the spring of 1904, Frank Fowler and his family moved to the canyon.

At the entrance of South Boulder Canyon were high vertical granite walls on either side. Fowler would call one side "Castle Rock" and the other "Twin Peaks." This rugged, picturesque location also had the advantage of easy access in a rolling countryside coming from the east. When the resort opened in July 1905, a lodge, swimming pool and tent city had been completed. Soon, small cabins began to spring up to accommodate tourists during the summer months.[208] The new Eldorado Hotel opened in 1908.

Ivy Baldwin's involvement with the Eldorado Springs resort, according to one report, came about as a result of his boast, as he flirted with some ladies, that he could walk a tightrope across the mouth of the canyon. This bragging reached the ears of resort owner Frank Fowler, who quickly seized on Baldwin's walk as sensational publicity.

"Are you sure you can do it?" Fowler asked.[209]

Always confident in his abilities, Ivy replied with an enthusiastic "yes." For his part, Baldwin, no doubt, saw an opportunity to earn money by continuing his death-defying exhibitions, capitalizing on one of his great and long-standing skills.

Fowler purchased a steel cable, nearly an inch thick, in Denver and then had it stretched from one canyon wall to the other, spanning the canyon gateway.[210] Some thirty-two guywires, stabilizing-type connections, were also attached to the rock walls. He needed access to the top of the cliffs, and he eventually constructed stairs, which he called the "Crazy Stairs." With these preparations, Fowler confidently claimed that this would be the highest walk in the world.

The 635-foot-long cable, when viewed from ground level, seemed almost invisible, as it was suspended 582 feet above the floor of the canyon.[211] Baldwin, in his walk on the high wire, appeared as a relatively small toy man. A "bead on a string," one writer called it. To be better seen, Ivy usually wore old white pants (which he called "lucky"), a white short-sleeved shirt and white socks. At an earlier time, he wore green tights, but now he disdained them as only appropriate for a circus. Personal equipment included a padded leather guard worn between his legs. He explained that if a tightrope walker fell, he would need to straddle the wire. Ivy used a 25-foot-long, twenty-four-pound balancing pole, which he grasped with a palm-outward hand on each side of the center and held at belly height.[212]

After climbing the stairs to the top of the canyon walls, he would take his camel hide shoes from a box, flex the soles and slip them on his small feet.[213] Then, with a steady gaze straight ahead, he would serenely and gracefully, in step-by-step cadence, glide across the wire to the awe and gasps of the numerous spectators. The trip across the canyon averaged approximately six minutes.

Aviator, Aerialist & Aeronaut

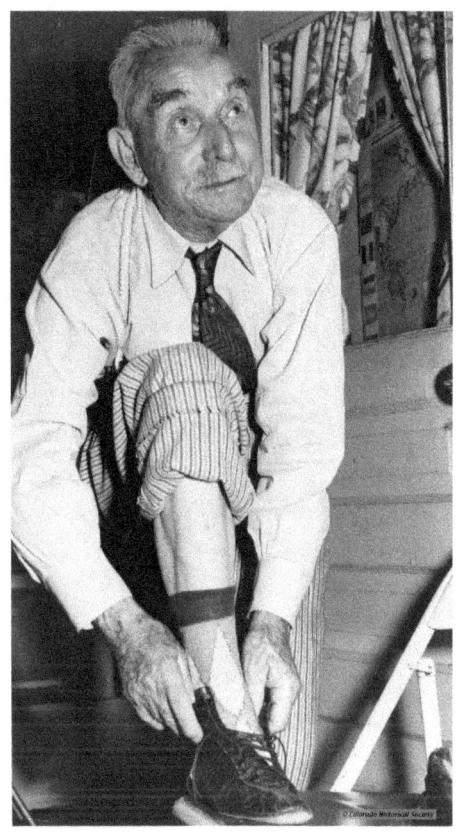

Left: Ivy Baldwin used special camel skin shoes in his tightrope walks, and this captures him changing his footwear. *History Colorado Collection.*

Below: This expanded postcard circulated widely during the time of Ivy Baldwin's death-defying tightrope walks across the mouth of South Boulder Canyon and above the Eldorado Springs resort. *Friends of Historic Fort Logan Archives.*

Colorado's Daring Ivy Baldwin

An Ivy tightrope walk always proved to be an astonishing feat, and it easily accomplished what Fowler had in mind in attracting visitors to the resort. A train began running from Denver to Eldorado Springs twice a day. The railroad publicized Ivy Baldwin walks in ads, which added many sightseers. The success of the walks and of the resort cemented a long business association and friendship between Ivy and the Fowler family.

Despite the height of the South Boulder Canyon walk, Ivy claimed that he was not scared. "I don't know that I have ever been real scared," he said. "I got a little bit while at the battle of Santiago some years ago, but I wouldn't say I was scared." Ivy maintained that all it takes to be a wire walker was a good sense of balance, "and that is something you don't lose."[214] Indeed, Baldwin was truly gifted with a great sense of balance, which, as he said, he never lost.

Left: Ivy Baldwin always astonished spectators with his ease of tightrope walking. Many viewers commented about the poise and grace that he demonstrated in his performances, whether high or low. *History Colorado Collection.*

Right: Ivy Baldwin possessed a great sense of balance and performed with remarkable concentration. His many fans saw his aerial skills as almost effortless. *History Colorado Collection.*

Looking down on the tightrope cable stretched across the entrance to South Boulder Canyon reveals the stabilizing guywires, helping Ivy Baldwin in his dramatic walks. *Carnegie Library for Local History, Boulder, Colorado.*

Ivy Baldwin (*white circle*) can barely be seen against the rugged rock walls of a Colorado canyon. *History Colorado Collection.*

Early on in his life, Ivy was inspired to do his walking by first noticing and then following the career of Charles Blondine. On several occasions, he said Blondine, the world-famous tightrope walker across Niagara Falls, had been a boyhood hero.

Ivy Baldwin seemed to impress the spectators with the ease with which he negotiated his walks, and he possessed an element of grace in his small frame that conveyed a sense of calm and confidence. But there were times when disaster appeared certain. After about the third or fourth time walking across the South Boulder Canyon, Ivy became blinded halfway across by the sun reflecting off the canyon wall. Unable to shake off the glare and his sudden blindness, Ivy calmly yelled at Fred Fowler and his brother, on the opposite cliff, to "start counting out loud, and keep right on counting." Ivy told the perplexed Fred Fowler that he was blinded and to continue counting loud and clear. The critical count, "one, two, three," continued until Ivy neared the rocky side. He instructed Fred to quickly and firmly grasp the balance pole with his hands when Ivy prepared to leap to the rock. Although Ivy safely gave his circus salute to the crowd as if nothing had happened, he remarked to his friends that he had never experienced that before. This episode led to voice guidance in such emergencies.[215]

On another frightening occasion, a sudden mountain storm with wind, rain and hail developed while Ivy was near the center of his walk. Buffeted by the elements, he had to hang by his knees and arms for nearly half an hour. Baldwin, on the cable, literally swayed in the wind until the storm subsided, and he was able to continue to the wall.[216]

While tightrope walking for a special event in the Cache La Poudre Canyon, nearer to Fort Collins, Colorado, Baldwin, at age sixty-eight, had a rare slip on the wire. Luckily, he caught the cable by his hands and had to finish the remaining sixty feet of the canyon by using his arms and legs wrapped around the wire. Some believed that a fierce gust of wind had nearly ended Ivy's life.[217]

Hazardous as the high wire canyon walks were, he always maintained that "the most dangerous walk of his life took place in 1885 in San Francisco."[218] Only nineteen at the time, he walked a wire from the Cliff House to Seal Rocks. He claimed the relatively low cable over the roiling Pacific water and the pounding surf made him dizzy, critically threatening his balance. Nevertheless, he performed this stunt a number of times, always impressing and pleasing the crowds.

These scary episodes in Ivy's tightrope walking were brushed aside as merely part of doing risky tricks. He not only continued his canyon walks for years but also graciously offered to perform for various community affairs. For example, at the age of seventy-nine, he walked a wire seventy feet above ground for a church benefit in Yuma, Colorado. When at home, he walked a low wire almost daily in his yard, sometimes entertaining kids.

Ivy never lost his sense of wanting to make the next exhibition more spectacular than the preceding one. In 1941, he announced his desire to walk across the Royal Gorge tourist site in central Colorado. This would entail an especially long wire walk at a still frightening height. His idea came to naught, however, because the Rio Grande Railroad, coursing through the gorge, nixed the thought. Ivy became "indignant at this interference." He asserted, "They were afraid the crowd below would get on the right-of-way at the tracks in the gorge and get hit by a train."[219]

While tightrope walks highlighted Ivy Baldwin's years after he abandoned flying airplanes, he continued performing balloon exhibitions, although less frequently. In September 1928, he made a parachute jump from a balloon at Denver Union Airport for the benefit of local aviators. News accounts reported that he dropped from an altitude of 1,200 feet, doing a "feat he had first performed 40 years ago."[220]

When the United States entered World War I in April 1917, Ivy sincerely believed his aviation experience would be of value to the American air service. Reports circulated in Denver that he had enlisted and that he had applied for a lieutenant's commission. Ivy's age of fifty-one, however, doomed this effort. Nevertheless, in March 1918, he kept trying. Newspapers stated that he had telegrammed Colorado senator John F. Shafroth, asking him to appeal to Secretary of War Newton Baker to allow enlistment in the aviation corps. This effort failed. The frustrated Ivy Baldwin said, "The airplane is going to win this war. They say I'm too old. Rot! I know all about airplanes as well as other craft that sail the sky. With my experience and skill, I believe I can be of service, and I want to go. I have two sons, fighting for Uncle Sam, and I want them to know that I am not the kind of daddy who sends his sons when he won't go himself."[221]

Also, about the time of World War I, Baldwin considered retirement, but he continued tightrope walks at Eldorado Springs until 1926. Two years later, he largely discontinued his daring work. He worked as a clerk at the Windsor Hotel and supervised billiard tables at the El Jebel shrine for some years. Keeping his interest in aviation alive, he worked as a watchman at old Lowry Field at Thirty-Eighth and Dahlia. The *Denver Post* reported on April 17, 1928, that Ivy had been the first person at Lowry, as a lookout, to spot the arrival of Charles Lindbergh's plane landing on a Sunday afternoon.²²² These other-than-entertainment jobs did not make Ivy Baldwin happy. He complained, "This quiet life is getting me down. I'll be getting old if I don't watch out."²²³ By 1928, Ivy Baldwin had made it known that he was retiring from more activities. He didn't find the reduced stunts satisfying either. "Sometimes I wish I were still risking my neck. There's nothing that beats it, so long as you don't get afraid. If you begin to get nervous, you'd better quit."²²⁴

As Ivy increasingly transitioned to a more quiet and slow-paced retirement, he and Bertha took up residence at Marshawn Park near Evergreen, Colorado. On many occasions, he would invite kids and guests to see him practice tightrope walking in his backyard, and he would, at times, open his big baggage chest and show off his prized silk kimono—a gift from the Japanese emperor.²²⁵ He would come to the resort swimming pool, and sometimes, when it became crowded, Ivy would do back flips off the diving board. Additionally, he enjoyed spinning a few yarns with resort visitors about his many career exploits.²²⁶ He was always the entertainer.

On December 10, 1947, Ivy's wife, Bertha, died at Presbyterian Hospital at the age of seventy-eight. His loving companion of fifty-four years, his great helper in constructing and repairing balloons and the mother of his

Ivy Baldwin demonstrated his acrobatic skills for patrons of the hot springs swimming pool at the Eldorado Springs resort. *Carnegie Library of Local History, Boulder, Colorado.*

three children had departed from his side. He was devastated. His two sons, Ira and Harry, had served in World War I and, afterward, became railroad men and moved away. Ira worked out of Ogden, Utah, for the Southern Pacific Railroad, while Harry worked as a conductor for the Denver and Rio Grande.[227] Daughter Ila, who had married Harry F. Newman and had two children, lived in the Denver area. She became more assertive in bringing a halt to Ivy's risky performances.

In August 1947, for example, Ila intervened when Ivy proposed to entertain his fellow Masonic El Jebel Temple members with a parachute leap at a family picnic at Elitch's. Ivy had to be content talking about his daredevil career.[228]

After Bertha's death, Ivy moved to a cabin at Eldorado Springs. Jack Fowler offered the accommodation to his longtime friend and employee.

Despite the family's opposition to Ivy's desire to perform some of his daring feats, there was still drama to come. As Ivy approached his eighty-second birthday on July 31, 1948, he pleaded with the Fowlers to let him do one more South Boulder Canyon tightrope walk to celebrate. Ivy had mentioned on several occasions that he had set a goal of walking across the canyon one hundred times. Although well short of that milestone, he remained determined that he could still walk the canyon wire when he was older than eighty, and he would demonstrate it. Jack Fowler, Frank Fowler's son and now in charge of the resort, declared Ivy was senile. He pointed out that Ivy hadn't done a walk for years. Ivy's daughter naturally opposed the idea. After some serious negotiating and some compromising, the opposition agreed to one final South Boulder Canyon tightrope walk but only at a height of 125 feet and 350 feet in length—one-fifth of the height of the soaring high cable. Even at this lower level and shorter distance, the walk would not lack for high excitement and a public dread for possibly seeing the worst outcome.

On July 31, 1948, Ivy's birthday, the Eldorado Springs resort was packed with a reported three thousand anxious spectators. Considerable publicity had alerted the public about Ivy Baldwin's final daring feat. The 108-pound Ivy donned his "lucky" white pants and initially wore a few old show items. He tossed off those robes, spat on his hands, rubbed them on his white pants, leaped over a railing, slipped on his camel-skin soled shoes and planted his feet on the wire. He momentarily grasped his balancing pole in one hand and waved to the crowd with the other. He took a few steps farther out on the wire and then—to the gasps and screams of the spectators—walked backward for a few short steps. The eighty-two-year-old Ivy Baldwin then

Aviator, Aerialist & Aeronaut

Above: Clad in white, Ivy Baldwin makes his final tightrope walk across the mouth of South Boulder Canyon to celebrate his eighty-second birthday. *History Colorado Collection.*

Left: Ivy Baldwin's celebration of his eighty-second birthday included this cake and a media event as part of his last canyon tightrope walk. *History Colorado Collection.*

calmly walked across and over the canyon. Gene Fowler, the former *Denver Post* journalist, wrote, "I didn't think he would make it when he climbed up to the wire, but, once he was on the wire and started across, he was his usual spectacular self."[229] The walk was a final, dramatic triumph for Ivy Baldwin. Reportedly, in a kind of anticlimax, he did it once more the following day to further prove his ability and skill.[230] That brought his total canyon crossings to eighty-eight.

A few years later, Ivy boasted, "I don't have to practice." He continued, "I could cross the canyon just as well today as I could 50 years ago."[231] But he had been "grounded for good" by his daughter and Jack Fowler. In reminiscing about his long career as a tightrope walker, he made the dubious assertion that if he "had it to do over again, he wouldn't be a wire walker." His point was that he could have made more money in some other business.[232] But Ivy Baldwin remained, to the end, a performer—a daredevil one at that. It would be hard to imagine him in a different career.

In September 1953, Ivy Baldwin went to Denver to address the Cactus Club. During that visit, he made his first appearance on television. The *Rocky Mountain News* said, "He was not fazed by the experience."[233]

On October 8, 1953, only a few days following Ivy's entrance into the television age, he unexpectedly died at his home in Eldorado Springs. The *Rocky Mountain News* commented, "The little man who had thrilled thousands with his casual strolls over yawning death, died in his sleep. He was 87."[234]

Jack Fowler, now managing the resort, stated that Baldwin had been in normal health and that the lights were still on in his cottage at 10:00 p.m., when Fowler had retired. "Apparently Mr. Baldwin got up sometime yesterday morning, Fowler said, and turned on his heat in his cottage. Then he returned to bed, as was his custom on cold mornings." The next morning, Harry Baldwin, Ivy's younger son, had come from the

Ivy Baldwin looks at his scrapbook during his final days. His cherished scrapbook provided important information about his entertaining career, particularly since he did not keep a diary or write letters. *History Colorado Collection.*

Aviator, Aerialist & Aeronaut

The Fowler family made this Eldorado Springs resort cabin available for Ivy during his late retirement, and he died there in his sleep at age eighty-seven. *History Colorado Collection.*

city of Arvada to visit and found him dead in bed. He believed his dad had suffered a heart attack.[235]

Ivy Baldwin, the little daredevil of tightrope walking, tower diving, balloon operations and airplane flying fame, had died in his bed. The thrilling showman and survivor of so many critical injuries quietly passed away at age eighty-seven.

IN PAUSING TO SURVEY the life of Ivy Baldwin, it becomes clear that in the decades spanning 1894 to 1953, he was very much a celebrity in the city of Denver. His name appeared frequently in the city newspapers and advertisements. Visitors to the amusement parks, most notably Elitch's Gardens, knew about his performances and eagerly paid to see his latest exhibitions. The parks crafted ads to lure spectators for particular events. Ivy Baldwin's name would be emphasized. His broad repertoire, balloon ascensions, trapeze acts, parachute drops, tower dives, piloting airplanes and tightrope walking greatly extended his reputation as a thrilling performer, with the added attraction of the public seeing something new and different. Unintentionally, Ivy's actual narrow escapes from death and his many injuries caused people to marvel at and talk about the courage, skills and, perhaps, luck of the little man. In sum, Ivy Baldwin was better known among the general populace than most other men.

Ivy Baldwin, from the beginning to the end, was an entertainer, showman and inventive performer. His fearlessness became legendary. His small stature likely contributed to a public perception that he was as a David doing battle with the Goliath of big challenges, performing in an event that could actually be life threatening. Although Baldwin reveled in the attention he received and was not above a boast now and then, he ably projected a rather quiet, confident and calm demeanor. Gene Fowler, an Ivy contemporary observer in his later years, praised a softer side of Baldwin's personality. "He was a kind, lovable little man who was especially fond of kids." He was "temperate in his living and his talk."[236] These characteristics combined to make him a popular figure.

Despite the lack of a formal education beyond the elementary level, Ivy sought to understand the rudimentary science associated with flying, whether with balloons or airplanes. He wanted to fly tests to explore air currents, lift characteristics and temperature effects. His consistent curiosity fueled by an energetic spirit prompted him to seek improvement in his and the army's balloons and their supporting equipment. Pragmatically, he borrowed designs for dirigibles and airplanes from others but made changes to adapt them to his situation. A major compensation for his lack of schooling came from his nationwide and worldwide travel. Since he always learned by doing, his international experiences gave him an unusual breadth of common-sense insights. They also provided fascinating tales for the entertainer. This was all the more remarkable, considering that he stated at one time that he had one fear: that of writing a letter—an indication that he did feel uncomfortable at times with his lack of formal schooling.[237]

Still another outstanding feature of Ivy Baldwin's life was the series of partnerships that he developed. The first one came when he became a virtual brother and partner with the Baldwin Brothers show. He learned about balloons, parachutes and show business from Thomas Baldwin. His teacher reigned as a powerful national aviation leader in many ways, and he served as an able guide for Ivy. A second partnership began quite early, with Denver's John and Mary Elitch. Ivy provided a profitable attraction for the Elitch's Gardens amusement park. At the same time, he gained extensive financial support for his exploits, which at times became costly disasters. That association proved mutually profitable. When Ivy enlisted in the army, he partnered with Captain Glassford in the development of the army's Signal

Corps balloon. And, of course, the last great partnership, based on Ivy's tightrope walking skills, emerged with the Fowler family and the Eldorado Springs resort. The Ivy Baldwin and Fowler business association continued, even as Ivy transitioned to a retired performer.

No effort has been made to detail or document Ivy's many injuries. Needless to say, they were numerous and, at times, life threatening. Some newspapers would claim that he had broken every bone in his body. Of particular note was the range of his injuries—from bruises and broken bones to serious burns. What remained remarkable was his recovery from so many ailments and his sustained courage to keep going. Ivy Baldwin's medical history could be a book in itself.

Any reviewer of Ivy's life cannot help but be impressed with the amazing records he compiled in sheer numbers. He had 2,500-plus balloon ascensions, 2,500-plus parachute drops,[238] 88 tightrope walks across the mouth of South Boulder Canyon and a reported 19 crashes in airplanes. The *Rocky Mountain News* colorfully observed, when Ivy was eighty-three, that "he's gone up in so many balloons his stomach still swings like a pendulum; and he'd walk a tight rope stretched over the pits of hell."[239] Added to these total numbers in various events were the important firsts: flying the first Colorado airship, flying the first Colorado seaplane and flying the first Nevada airplane. In 1969, the Colorado Aviation Historical Society posthumously selected Baldwin as the first inductee in the Colorado Aviation Hall of Fame. University of Colorado history professor Scamehorn said Ivy Baldwin should be remembered as "the central figure of aeronautics in the West."[240]

In a final word, Ivy Baldwin should not only be remembered as a consummate aerialist and a widely known celebrity of the late and early decades of the nineteenth and twentieth centuries but also as a significant pioneering man of aviation in Colorado and the West.

NOTES

Preface

1. White, *Compound Fractures*. This 2013 crime novel uses Ivy Baldwin's sensational across-canyon tightrope walks as a metaphor.

Chapter 1

2. Scamehorn, "First Fifty Years of Flight," 104.
3. *Houston Herald*, August 31, 1896. In 1896, Ivy's brothers, John F.Y. and Ridell, with his mother, still lived in Houston.
4. Fowler, *Solo in Tom Toms*, 207.
5. McCoy, "Adventures of Ivy Baldwin," 5. This article reported on an interview with Ivy Baldwin in September 1953.
6. Publications vary on the date Ivy ran away from home. Scamehorn, in "First Fifty Years of Flight," says he left at the age of ten. In the Ivy Baldwin September 1953 interview, he said he was thirteen when he ran away from home.
7. Jean Michel, interview by author, November 8, 2017.
8. Crouch, *Eagle Aloft*, 510.
9. Ibid., 512.
10. Fowler, *Solo in Tom Toms*, 202–03.
11. Ibid. Some sources said Ivy's first balloon ascension was in Evansville, Indiana, in 1879. This date might be suspicious, since Ivy was only thirteen at the time.

12. Ibid.
13. *Houston Daily Post*, 1905.
14. Crouch, *Eagle Aloft*, 505.
15. Ibid. Scamehorn indicates that Ivy also used a professional name of William DeIvy at one time.
16. Ibid., 507.
17. Scamehorn, "Thomas Scott Baldwin," 163–76; *Rocky Mountain News*, "Dare-Devil Was Aviation Pioneer," October 29, 1967. Scamehorn states the Cliff House walk was four hundred feet.
18. Ibid.
19. Ibid.
20. McCoy, "Adventures of Ivy Baldwin," 4.
21. Ibid.
22. Scamehorn, "Thomas Scott Baldwin," 173.
23. Parkinson, "Benjamin Franklin on Aeronautics," 246; Bigelow, *Complete Works of Benjamin Franklin*.
24. McCoy, "Adventures of Ivy Baldwin," 4.
25. Scamehorn, *Balloons to Jets*, 11.
26. McCoy, "Adventures of Ivy Baldwin," 4.
27. *Quincy Herald Whig*.
28. McCoy, "Adventures of Ivy Baldwin," 5.
29. Crouch, *Eagle Aloft*, 507.
30. *Rocky Mountain News*, August 10, 1949.
31. McCoy, "Adventures of Ivy Baldwin," 5–6.
32. Ibid., 4.
33. *Rocky Mountain News*, August 10, 1949. Another newspaper, on June 21, 1928, said Ivy had had "4,000 leaps."
34. McCoy, "Adventures of Ivy Baldwin," 4.
35. Crouch, *Eagle Aloft*, 509–10.
36. Bacon, *Dominion of the Air*, 255.
37. Crouch, *Eagle Aloft*, 510.

Chapter 2

38. *Rocky Mountain News*, "America's Most Distinctive Amusement Park, Elitchs, Denver, Colorado, 75 Years of Fun," June 19, 1966, advertising supplement.
39. Fowler, *Solo in Tom Toms*, 197.
40. *Rocky Mountain News*, May 22, 1890.

41. Ibid., May 31, 1890.
42. Scamehorn, "First Fifty Years of Flight," 104.
43. Crouch, *Eagle Aloft*, 515.
44. Ibid.
45. *Denver Daily News*, November 12, 1894.
46. McCoy, "Adventures of Ivy Baldwin," 6.
47. *Denver Daily News*, November 12, 1894.
48. McCoy, "Adventures of Ivy Baldwin," 6.
49. Ibid.
50. *Denver Republican*, June 15, 1913.
51. Ibid.
52. Crouch, *Eagle Aloft*, 516.
53. Ibid.
54. McCoy, "Adventures of Ivy Baldwin," 11.
55. Scamehorn, "Thomas Scott Baldwin," 174.
56. *Quincy Daily Journal*, September 24, 1891.
57. Crouch, *Eagle Aloft*, 516; Scamehorn, "Thomas Scott Baldwin," 174–75.
58. *Anglo-American*, February 12, 1892.
59. Ibid.
60. *Quincy Daily Herald*, October 2, 1892.
61. *Mexico City Two Republics*, February 22, 1892.
62. *Anglo-American*, February 27, 1892.
63. *Denver Daily News*, November 12, 1894.
64. Ibid., April 18, 1892.
65. Ibid.
66. *Mexico City Two Republics*, May 17, 1892.
67. *Anglo-American*, May 25, 1892.
68. McCoy, "Adventures of Ivy Baldwin," 12.
69. Ibid.
70. *Quincy Daily Herald*, October 1, 1892.
71. Ibid., July 6, 1892.
72. *Chicago Times*, October 2, 1892.
73. *Quincy Daily Herald*, October 3, 1892.
74. *Mexico City Two Republics*, January 3, 1893.
75. *Anglo-American*, January 29, 1893.
76. Ibid.
77. Ibid.
78. *Denver Daily News*, August 31, 1896.
79. *Mexico City Two Republics*, January 31, 1893.

80. *Quincy Daily Whig*, February 15, 1893.
81. Ibid.
82. *Quincy Daily Herald*, April 18, 1893.
83. Scamehorn, "Thomas Scott Baldwin," 175.
84. *Anglo-American*, April 18, 1892.
85. *Quincy Daily Herald*, July 5, 1893.
86. Crouch, *Eagle Aloft*, 518. The marriage occurred in 1892.
87. *Colorado Evening Sun*, August 9, 1893.
88. *Stockton Evening Mail*, September 18, 1893.
89. *Quincy Daily Herald*, October 10, 1893.
90. Ibid.
91. *San Francisco Chronicle*, February 3, 1894.
92. Ibid.
93. *Quincy Daily Herald*, October 10, 1893.

Chapter 3

94. *Denver Daily News*, August 3, 1894.
95. Ibid.
96. *Rocky Mountain News*, August 19, 1894. This detailed account was written by Harry H. Buckwalter. He referred to himself in the article as the "News Reporter."
97. Ibid.
98. Ibid.
99. Ibid.
100. Ibid.
101. *Denver Daily News*, August 13, 1894. Buckwalter's balloon flight experience had some similarities to that of Major General Fitz-John Porter during the Civil War. General Porter's balloon broke free of tethering and drifted over Confederate positions but luckily drifted back over Federal lines before he crashed.
102. *Denver Daily News*, September 17, 1894.
103. Ibid., November 12, 1894.
104. Ibid.
105. Ibid.
106. Ibid.
107. Ibid.
108. Ibid.

109. Ibid.
110. Ibid., January 7, 1895.
111. Ibid.
112. Ibid.
113. Davis, "Air Role in the War," 13–29; Emerson, "Great Weapon or 'Fanciful Contraption,'" 33–38.
114. Report of the Chief Signal Officer, H.R. Rep. 52 (1891).
115. Ullman, "War Balloon Santiago," 119.
116. During the Chicago exhibition, a notable communication step beyond the telegraph occurred with a telephone message from balloon to ground.
117. Ullman, "War Balloon Santiago," 119.
118. Ibid.; Hennessy, "Balloons and Airships," 38–49. Captain Glassford reportedly had an office in Denver's Equitable Building, where he displayed models of some foreign balloons.
119. *Denver Daily News*, December 4, 1897, Ivy Baldwin Scrapbook.
120. *Denver Evening Post*, May 9, 1895.
121. Ibid.; Hennessy, "Balloons and Airships," 45. Ivy Baldwin, in a later letter to a friend, claimed the gas used in the General Myer had not been washed and dried properly before using it in the balloon, and the hot gas had rotted the goldbeater skin when the balloon arrived at Fort Logan.
122. Ullman, "War Balloon Santiago," 120.
123. *New York Times*, September 1, 1895.
124. Fowler, *Solo in Tom Toms*, 198. Fowler said Bertha, Ivy and son Harry worked on constructing balloons (twenty-nine feet across) of muslin and used a "dope" made of molasses, sulphur, flour, yellow ochre and alum.
125. Ullman, "War Balloon Santiago," 120, 129.
126. *Denver Daily News*, August 31, 1896. The paper also stated, "This is the first serious accident he had ever had and was one of the most unexpected that could have happened."
127. Ibid.
128. *Houston Herald*, August 31, 1896.
129. *Denver Daily News*, August 31, 1896.
130. Ibid., August 28, 1897.
131. Ullman, "War Balloon Santiago," 120–21.

Chapter 4

132. *Annual Report of the Department of the Colorado.*

133. Ullman, "War Balloon Santiago," 127.
134. *Denver Daily News*, April 4, 1898.
135. Ibid.
136. Hennessy, "Balloons and Airships," 45.
137. Ullman, "War Balloon Santiago," 122. An additional officer joined the unit before landing in Cuba.
138. Ibid.
139. *Quincy Morning Whig*, November 4, 1898.
140. Ibid.
141. Ullman, "War Balloon Santiago," 123.
142. Ibid., 124.
143. *Quincy Morning Whig*, October 28, 1898.
144. Ibid., November 4, 1898.
145. Friedel, *Splendid Little War*, 150.
146. *Quincy Morning Whig*, November 4, 1898.
147. Ullman, "War Balloon Santiago," 128.
148. Ibid., 126.
149. *Daily Bee*, October 4, 1898.
150. Ullman, "War Balloon Santiago," 128.
151. *Quincy Morning Whig*, November 4, 1898, Ivy Baldwin Scrapbook.
152. Hennessy, "Balloons and Airships," 46.
153. Ullman, "War Balloon Santiago," 128.

Chapter 5

154. *Denver Times*, July 14, 1901.
155. Fowler, *Solo in Tom Toms*, 199.
156. *Denver Post*, July 24, 1901.
157. Ibid., July 25, 1901.
158. Ibid., July 28, 1901.
159. Ibid., July 29, 1901.
160. *Denver Times*, August 9, 1901.
161. Ibid., August 12, 1901.
162. Ibid., August 14, 1901.
163. Ibid., August 19, 1901.
164. Ibid., August 26, 1901.
165. *Denver Post*, October 28, 1901.

166. Jones and Jones, *Buckwalter*; *Denver Times*, October 22, 1901; August 28, 1901.
167. *Arvada Harvest*, September 2, 1948.
168. *Denver Post*, May 27, 1902.
169. Ibid., August 3, 1902.
170. Ibid.
171. Ibid., September 2, 1902; August 24, 1902. The later stated that Big Glory had a diameter of 65 feet, circumference of 204 feet and gas capacity of 140,000 cubic feet.
172. 1930 United States Census.
173. *Denver Post*, August 25, 1907.
174. Ibid., August 16, 1909.
175. Ibid.

Chapter 6

176. Crouch, *Eagle Aloft*, 528. Tom Baldwin's 1908 dirigible was accepted by the army nearly a full year before the Wright airplane, becoming America's first powered military aircraft. A steerable balloon, a dirigible, was first developed by Jules Henri Gifford in 1852.
177. Scamehorn, "First Fifty Years of Flight," 108. This gives the airship length as fifty-seven feet, the gas capacity as twenty-two thousand pounds and the motor horsepower as eight. He rated the speed as only five miles per hour.
178. *Denver Post*, May 13, 1906.
179. Ibid.
180. Scamehorn, "First Fifty Years of Flight," 107.
181. Ibid., 108; *Denver Post*, June 19, 1906.
182. This dramatic account was contained in a story in the *Kansas City Journal*, October 7, 1906.
183. Scamehorn, "First Fifty Years of Flight," 108–09.
184. *Houston Daily Post*, in Ivy Baldwin Scrapbook.
185. Ibid.
186. Crouch, *Eagle Aloft*, 529.
187. Scamehorn, "First Fifty Years of Flight," 113.
188. *Denver Post*, July 30, 1909.
189. Ibid.

190. Ibid., July 31, 1909.
191. Ibid., July 30, 1909.
192. Ibid., August 7, 1909.
193. Ibid.
194. Ibid., August 5, 1909.
195. Ibid.
196. Ibid., July 31, 1909.
197. Ibid., February 2, 3, 4, 1910.
198. Scamehorn, "First Fifty Years of Flight," 102.
199. McCoy, "Adventures of Ivy Baldwin," 10.
200. *Denver Republican*, June 15, 1913.
201. Publication of the Nevada Aerospace Hall of Fame, http://www.nahof.org.
202. Ibid. The next month, Walter Brookins set a new flight altitude record of 6,175 feet.
203. *Denver Post*, May 19, 1913. The headline read, "Birdman Baldwin Gets Ducking at Manhattan Beach"; Scamehorn, "First Fifty Years of Flight," 116.
204. *Denver Republican*, June 15, 1913.
205. McCoy, "Adventures of Ivy Baldwin," 10.

Chapter 7

206. *Rocky Mountain News*, August 16, 1941. Various newspaper articles differed on the total of the South Boulder Canyon crossings. Totals ranged from eighty-two to eighty-nine. Ivy claimed eighty-six crossings, but that total did not include two on his eighty-second birthday.
207. *Boulder Daily Camera*, June 11, 1972.
208. Fowler, *Solo in Tom Toms*, 181–82.
209. Empire Magazine, *Denver Post*, May 28, 1974; Fowler, *Solo in Tom Toms*. Gene Fowler simply writes that Frank Fowler had the idea of a cable across the canyon mouth and then recruited Ivy Baldwin to do the walk. Frank Fowler knew that only one man could do it, and that was Ivy Baldwin.
210. Some newspapers stated the cable was 3/8 inches and others 7/8 inches.
211. The length and height of the cable across the mouth of South Boulder Canyon varied in many reports and advertisements. The measurements listed here were most frequently quoted. Robert Ripley of *Believe It or Not* fame once reported the height as "the highest tightrope walk in the world."

212. Some newspapers claimed the pole weighed twenty-six pounds.
213. Fowler, *Solo in Tom Toms*, 203. The camel hide shoes were used, said Ivy, because they don't get slippery when wet.
214. *Rocky Mountain News*, September 9, 1953.
215. Fowler, *Solo in Tom Toms*, 205–06; *Rocky Mountain News*, October 9, 1953.
216. Ibid.
217. *Arvada Harvest*, September 2, 1948.
218. *Rocky Mountain News*, undated clipping in Denver Public Library clipping file.
219. Ibid., August 16, 1941.
220. Unidentified newspaper clipping in the Denver Pubic Library clipping file.
221. Unidentified newspaper clipping, March 24, 1918, in Denver Public Library clipping file.
222. *Denver Post*, April 17, 1928.
223. *Rocky Mountain News*, August 16, 1941.
224. Ibid. For a period of time in 1929, Ivy and Bertha went to Phoenix on a doctor's suggestion, but they soon returned to Denver.
225. Michel interview.
226. Empire Magazine, *Denver Post*, July 28, 1974.
227. Unidentified newspaper clipping in the Denver Public Library clipping file.
228. *Rocky Mountain News*, August 10, 1949.
229. Ibid., October 9, 1953.
230. Ibid., September 20, 1972.
231. Ibid., September 9, 1953.
232. Rogers, "Walking the High Wire," 14. Reports differed on what Ivy Baldwin earned in his tightrope walking. One source said he was paid $100 for each walk while other sources claimed he got up to 50 percent of the gate receipts.
233. *Rocky Mountain News*, September 9, 1953.
234. Ibid., October 9, 1953.
235. Ibid.
236. Ibid.
237. Fowler, *Solo in Tom Toms*, 192.
238. *Rocky Mountain News*, September 20, 1972; Empire Magazine, *Denver Post*, July 28, 1974.
239. *Rocky Mountain News*, August 10, 1949.
240. Ibid., October 29, 1967; Lawson, "Life on a High Wire." The cable across the entrance to South Boulder Canyon remained in place until 1974, when its anchors were blasted from the rock.

SELECTED BIBLIOGRAPHY

Adler, Irene. *Ballooning: High and Wild*. Mahwah, NJ: Troll Associates, 1976.
The American Heritage History of Flight. New York: Simon and Schuster, 1962.
Anglo-American. 1892–93.
Annual Report of the Department of the Colorado. Appendix M. Office of the Signal Corps. August 15, 1898.
Arvada Harvest. August 15, 1898.
Bacon, J.M. *The Dominion of the Air: The Story of Aerial Navigation*. N.p.: David McKay, 1903.
Berget, Alphonse. *The Conquest of the Air*. New York: G.P. Putnam's Sons, 1911.
Bigelow, John, ed. *The Complete Works of Benjamin Franklin*. New York: G.P. Putnam's Sons, 1888.
Block, Eugene. *Above the Civil War: The Story of Thaddeus Lowe, Balloonist, Inventor, Railway Builder*. Berkeley, CA: Howell-North Books, 1966.
Botting, Douglas. *The Grand Airships*. New York: Time-Life Books, 1980.
Boulder Daily Camera. 1972.
Canby, Courtlandt. *A History of Flight*. London: Hawthorn Books, Inc., 1963.
Chandler, Charles de Forest. *How Our Army Grew Wings: Airmen and Aircraft before 1914*. New York: Ronald Press Company, 1926.
Chicago Times. 1892.
Colorado Evening Sun. 1893.
Crouch, Tom D. *The Eagle Aloft: Two Centuries of the Balloon in America*. Washington, D.C.: Smithsonian Institution Press, 1983.

Selected Bibliography

Daily Bee. 1898.
Davis, Captain Daniel T. "The Air Role in the War Between the States." *Air University Review* 27, no. 5 (July–August 1976): 13–29.
Denver Daily News. 1894–97.
Denver Evening Post. 1895.
Denver Post. 1901–74.
Denver Republican. 1913.
Denver Times. 1901.
Dwiggins, Don. *Riders of the Winds: The Story of Ballooning.* London: Hawthorn Books, 1973.
Ege, Lennart. *Balloons and Airships.* New York: Macmillan, 1974.
Emerson, Jason. "Great Weapon or 'Fanciful Contraption'?" *Civil War Times*, December 2012.
Emme, Eugene M., ed. *Two Hundred Years of Flight in America: A Bicentennial Survey.* San Diego, CA: Unnelt, Inc., 1977.
Fowler, Gene. *A Solo in Tom Toms.* London: Viking Press, 1946.
Friedel, Frank. *The Splendid Little War.* Boston: Little Brown & Co., 1958.
Greely, General A.W. "Balloons in War." *Harper's Monthly Magazine* 101, no. 601.
Haydon, F. Stansbury. *Aeronautics in the Union and Confederate Armies.* Vol. I. Baltimore, MD: Johns Hopkins Press, 1941.
Heinmuller, John P.N. *Man's Fight to Fly.* New York: Aero Print Co., 1945.
Hennessey, Juliette A. "Balloons and Airships: The United States Army Air Arm, April 1861 to April 1917." *Aerospace Historian* 17, no. 1 (Spring 1970).
History of Eldorado Springs. Colorado Division of Parks and Outdoor Recreation. March 1980.
Hoehling, Mary. *Thaddeus Lowe: America's One Man Air Corps.* Chicago: Kingston House, 1958.
Houston Herald. 1896.
Jackson, Donald Dale. *The Aeronauts.* New York: Time-Life Books, 1980.
Jones, William C., and Elizabeth B. Jones. *Buckwalter: The Colorado Scenes of a Pioneering Photojournalist, 1890–1920.* Boulder, CO: Pruett Publishing Company, 1989.
Kansas City Journal. 1906.
Lawson, Kathy. "Life on a High Wire." *Images Magazine.*
McCoy, Earl. "Adventures of Ivy Baldwin, Aerialist." *Denver Westerners Roundup* 48 (March–April 1993): 3–12.
Mexico City Two Republics. 1892–93.
Milbank, Jeremiah, Jr. *The First Century of Flight in America.* Princeton, NJ: Princeton University Press, 1943.

Selected Bibliography

New York Times. November 13, 1894; February 4, 1895; February 13, 1896.
Parkin, J.H. *Bell and Baldwin.* Toronto, ON: University of Toronto, 1964.
Parkinson, Russell J. "Benjamin Franklin on Aeronautics." *Airpower Historian* 6, no. 4 (October 1959): 245–47.
Pendergast, Curtis. *The First Aviators.* New York: Time-Life Books, 1980.
Pettem, Silvia. *Only in Boulder: The County's Colorful Characters.* Charleston, SC: The History Press, 2010.
Pineau, Roger. *Ballooning, 1782–1972.* Washington, D.C.: Smithsonian Institution Press, 1972.
Publication of the Nevada Aerospace Hall of Fame. http://www.nahof.org.
Quincy Daily Herald. 1892–93.
Quincy Daily Journal. 1891.
Quincy Daily Whig.
Quincy Herald Whig.
Quincy Morning Whig. 1898.
Report of the Chief Signal Officer. H.R. Rep. 52 (1891).
Rocky Mountain News. 1890–1972.
Rogers, Maria. "Walking the High Wire." *Senior Voice*, September 1995.
Rolt, L.T.C. *The Aeronauts: A History of Ballooning, 1783–1903.* New York: Walker and Company, 1966.
Rotch, Abbott Lawrence. *Benjamin Franklin and the First Balloons.* Worcester, MA: Davis Press, 1907.
Sampson, Joanna. *A Glimpse at Eldorado's Colorful Past.* Eldorado Springs, CO: Eldorado Canyon State Park, 1997.
San Francisco Chronicle. 1894.
Scamehorn, Howard L. *Balloons to Jets.* Chicago: Henry Regnery Company, 1957.
———. "The First Fifty Years of Flight in Colorado." *University of Colorado Bulletin* no. 2. History Series. 1966.
———. "Thomas Scott Baldwin: The Columbus of the Air." *Illinois State Historical Society Journal* 49, no. 2 (Summer 1956): 163–89.
Scrivner, John H. "The Military Use of Balloons and Dirigibles in the United States, 1793–1963." Master's diss., University of Oklahoma, 1963.
Simmonds, Ralph. *All About Airships.* New York: Doran Company, 1911.
Stockton Evening Mail. 1893.
Ullman, Bruce L. "The War Balloon Santiago." *Aerospace Historian* 32, no. 2 (Summer/June 1985): 107–16.
White, Stephen. *Compound Fractures.* New York: Dutton, 2013.
Wragg, David W. *Flight before Flying.* New York: Frederick Fell Publishers, 1974.

INDEX

A

Abbott, Wayne 65
Ady, George C. 71, 72
Aero Club 71
Alexander Palace 17
Army of the Potomac 41
Arvada, Colorado 89
Asia 17, 20, 23, 33

B

Baker, Newton 84
Baldwin Brothers 11, 15, 17, 18, 19, 23, 30, 31, 90
Baldwin, Harry E. 64
Baldwin, Helen (Ila) 64
Baldwin, Ira W. 40, 86
Baldwin Park 23, 27, 30
Baldwin, Samuel Yates (Sam) 11
Baldwin, Thomas Scott (Tom) 11, 12, 14, 15, 17, 18, 19, 20, 23, 28, 40, 64, 66, 90
Balloon Society of Great Britain 17
Baltimore, Maryland 7
Banks, Sir Joseph 12
Barnum, P.T. 19

Battle of Fair Oaks 41
Big Glory (balloon) 64
Blondine, Charles 83
Bowen, Ben 60
Briggsville 27
Brookins, Walter 73
Brown, Eugene 27
Buckwalter, Harry H. 37

C

Cache La Poudre Canyon 83
Cactus Club 88
Calcutta, India 22
California Arrow 66, 67
Cape Verde Islands 49
Carson City, Nevada 74
Carson City Sagebrush Carnival 74
Castaneda 25, 26, 28
Castle Rock 57, 77
Central America 24
Cervera, Admiral Pascual 49
China 22
Civil War 41, 42
Cliff House 11, 83
Cloud Swing 32

Index

Code of Balloon Tactics 43
Colorado and Southern Railroad 59
Colorado National Guard 64
"Columbus of the Air" 11
Coney Island of Mexico 25
Crane, Stephen 52
Cuba 48, 50, 51, 54, 55
Curtiss 66, 73, 74
Curtiss-Paulhan 74

D

Daiquiri 51
Denver, Colorado 7, 8, 19, 20, 31, 32, 33, 35, 37, 38, 39, 40, 41, 42, 43, 44, 47, 49, 50, 55, 56, 57, 60, 64, 70, 71, 72, 73, 74, 75, 77, 78, 80, 84, 86, 88, 89, 90
Denver Union Airport 84
Department of the Colorado 39, 40, 42, 48
Derby, Lieutenant Colonel George 51
Díaz, President Porfirio 30
Douglas County 57

E

El Caney 51
Eldorado Hotel 78
Eldorado Springs, Colorado 76, 77, 78, 80, 84, 86, 88, 91
Elitch (airship) 67, 68, 69
Elitch, John 19, 20, 31, 67, 90
Elitch, Mary 90
Elitch's Gardens 20, 31, 35, 37, 44, 56, 57, 60, 64, 65, 67, 71, 72, 75, 89, 90
El Jebel 84, 86
El Pozo 51, 52
Evergreen, Colorado 85

F

Farina, G.A. 17

Farman III (aircraft) 73
First Balloon Company 53
Florence, Colorado 64
Fort Collins, Colorado 83
Fort Logan 8, 39, 40, 42, 43, 44, 47, 48, 49, 55
Fort Myer 54, 55
Fort Riley 42
Fort Wadsworth 48, 49, 50
Fowler, Frank 77, 78, 86
Fowler, Fred 83
Fowler, Gene 10, 88, 90
Fowler, Jack 86
France 12, 41, 48, 54, 73
Franco-Prussian War 42
Franklin, Benjamin 12
Frazier, Fred 44

G

General Aviation Company 75, 76
General Castillo 51
General Myer 41, 42, 43, 44
Georgetown, Colorado 59, 60
Georgetown Loop 60
Glassford, Captain William A. 39
Golden, Colorado 60
Golden Gate 73, 74
Golden Gate Park 17
Goodwater Grove 32
Great Britain 17, 18
Greely, Brigadier General Adolphus W. 39, 40, 41, 42, 54, 55

H

Haywood, Private 53
Hearst, William Randolph 48
Henderson 38
Hong Kong 22
Houston, Texas 9, 10, 11, 47, 70
Hoxsey, Arch 73
Hudson, Percy 64

INDEX

I

Ivy, Elizabeth 9
Ivy, John H. 9
Ivy, William 9, 11, 12, 17, 18

J

Jackson, M.A. 24
Japan 34
Japanese emperor 22, 85
Java 22, 23
John Elitch's Zoological Gardens 19
Johnston, Ralph 73

K

Kansas City, Missouri 68
Knabenshue, A. Roy 66

L

Lake Texcoco 25
Laredo, Texas 30
Lindbergh, Charles 84
Lopez, Fadrique 28
Lowe, Thaddeus S.C. 41
Lowry Field 84

M

Madras, India 22
Maine (battleship) 49
Manhattan Beach 44, 60, 75, 76
Marr, W.L. 73
MARS 27
Marshawn Park 85
Mathews, Jim 69
Mathewson, E. Linn 73
Maxfield, Joseph E. 42
McClellan, General George B. 41
McCook, Major General Alexander M. 39, 40, 41, 42
McKinley, President William 49
Meigs, Quartermaster General M.C. 41

Memorial Day 20
Mexico 20, 23, 25, 26, 27, 28, 30, 31
Mexico City, Mexico 19, 23, 24, 25, 27
Midwinter Exposition 32
Miles, Major General Nelson A. 43
Moffat Lakes Resort Company 77
Monaco Boulevard 73
Montgolfier brothers 12
Myer, Dr. A.J. 42

N

Nadar 38
Nagasaki, Japan 20
Nevada 74, 76, 91
Nevada Aerospace Hall of Fame 74
Newman, Harry F. 86
Niagara Falls 83

O

Oakland's Idora Park 66
Ogden, Utah 86
Old Glory (balloon) 60
Omaha, Nebraska 54, 55
Oregon 72

P

Parker 57
Park Hill 73
Paulhan, Louis 73
Pedro Springs, Texas 10
"Pictures from the Sky" 35
Pike's Peak 64
Pulitzer, Joseph 48

Q

Quincy, Illinois 7, 8, 11, 12, 15, 17, 23, 27, 30, 31, 33, 34, 39, 48, 54

INDEX

R

Rangoon 22
Raycraft Ranch 74
Rio Grande Railroad 84
Rio Grande (ship) 51
Rocky Mountain News 19, 77, 88, 91
Roosevelt, Thoeodore 54
Rough Riders 54
Royal Gorge 84

S

Saigon 22
Salt Lake City, Utah 73
San Angel 25
San Antonio River 10
San Antonio, Texas 10, 77
San Francisco 7, 11, 14, 17, 20, 32, 33, 50, 73, 74, 83
San Francisco Bay 66
San Jose, California 66
San Juan Hill 51, 52, 54, 70
San Luis Potosi 26
Santiago 50, 51, 52, 53, 54, 64, 80
Santiago (balloon) 52, 53, 54
Seal Rock 11
Second Balloon Company 54
secretary of war 39, 42, 84
Sells Brothers Circus 10
Shafroth, Senator John F. 84
Shafter, Major General William R. 50, 51
Shanghai, China 22
Sherman, Bertha Louise 31
Sibley, Frank P. 56
Siboney 51, 53
Signal Corps 39, 41, 42, 44, 47, 49, 50, 53, 54, 55, 64, 91
Singapore 22
Singleton Park 15
South America 24
South Boulder Canyon 77, 80, 83, 86, 91
Southern Pacific Railroad 86

Spain 49
Spencer, Percival 20
SS *City of Peking* 20
Stockton, California 31, 32

T

Table Mountain 60
Tampa, Florida 50, 51
Terre Haute, Indiana 10
Thayer-Noyes Circus 10
"The Aeronaut" 24
Thumb, Mr. and Mrs. Tom 19
Tivoli Ermita 26
Tivoli San Cosmo 28
Tizapan 26
Tokyo, Japan 20, 21, 22
Trans-Mississippi and International Exhibition 54

U

Uyeno Park 20

V

Van Tassel, Park A. 14
Vladivostok, Russia 22
Volkmar, Lieutenant W.S. 51

W

Wager, Arthur C. 75
Washington (balloon) 41
Washington, D.C. 39
West Indies 24
Wichita Falls, Texas 10
World Columbian Exposition 42
World War I 84, 86
Wright brothers 65, 70, 72, 73, 75

Y

Yuma, Colorado 84

ABOUT THE AUTHOR

Jack Stokes Ballard holds a doctorate of philosophy in American history from University of California, Los Angeles, taught history at the Air Force Academy and AFROTC at Occidental College, served a career in the air force and retired as chief of the plans and requirements division at Lowry Air Force Base. He worked for the Martin Marietta Corporation for twelve years. He is the author of eight books.

Visit us at
www.historypress.com

www.ingramcontent.com/pod-product-compliance
Lightning Source LLC
Chambersburg PA
CBHW042141160426
43201CB00021B/2364